SERIES EDITOR: **Roger Porkess**

Formula One
MATHS Gold

B

Susan Ball ● Dave Blackman

Margaret Bland ● Sophie Goldie

Abigail Kent ● Katie Porkess

Susan Terry ● Leonie Turner

Brandon Wilshaw ●

Hodder & Stoughton

A MEMBER OF THE HODDER HEADLINE GROUP

Acknowledgements

Every effort has been made to trace and acknowledge ownership of copyright. The publishers will be glad to make suitable arrangements with any copyright holder whom it has not been possible to contact.

Illustrations were drawn by Maggie Brand, Jeff Edwards and Claire Philpott.

Photos
page 12 © CORBIS SYGMA
page 27 © BDI Images
page 82 © Geoscience Features Picture Library, Dr Basil Booth
page 110 Ralph A. Clevenger/CORBIS
page 111 © 2001 Cordon Art-Baarn-Holland. All rights reserved
page 167 © SCIENCE SOURCE/SCIENCE PHOTO LIBRARY
page 204, left and centre © Roger Ressmeyer/CORBIS
page 204, right © Dallas and John Heaton/CORBIS
page 210 © Galen Rowell/CORBIS

Maps
page 29 Reproduced by kind permission of Ordnance Survey © Crown Copyright
NC/A7/04/25629

Cover design and page design by Julie Martin.

Orders: please contact Bookpoint Ltd, 130 Milton Park, Abingdon, Oxon OX14 4SB. Telephone: (44) 01235 827720.
Fax: (44) 01235 400454. Lines are open from 9.00–6.00, Monday to Saturday, with a 24-hour message answering service.
You can also order through our website www.madaboutbooks.co.uk.

British Library Cataloguing in Publication Data
A catalogue record for this title is available from The British Library

ISBN 0 340 86933X

First published 2004
Impression number   10 9 8 7 6 5 4 3 2 1
Year   2010 2009 2008 2007 2006 2005 2004

Copyright © 2004 Susan Ball, Dave Blackman, Margaret Bland, Sophie Goldie, Abigail Kent, Katie Porkess, Roger Porkess, Susan Terry, Leonie Turner, Brandon Wilshaw

Cover photo from Jacey, Debut Art

Typeset by Tech-Set Ltd, Gateshead, Tyne & Wear
Printed in Italy for Hodder & Stoughton Educational, a division of Hodder Headline Plc, 338 Euston Road, London NW1 3BH

Introduction

This book is designed for Year 8 students working at Levels 3 to 4 of the National Curriculum, and is accompanied by a substantial Teacher's Resource. Books A and C cover Years 7 and 9. These three *Gold* books are an integral part of the *Formula One Maths* series and may be used alongside books A1, B1 and C1 during the three years of Key Stage 3.

The series builds on the National Numeracy Strategy in primary schools and its extension into Key Stage 3. It is designed to support that style of teaching and the lesson framework.

This book is presented as a series of double-page spreads, each of which is designed to be a lesson. The left-hand page covers the material to be taught and the right-hand page provides questions and activities for the students to work through. Each chapter ends with a 'Finishing off' Review exercise covering all its content. Further worksheets, tests and ICT materials are provided in the Teacher's Resource. Answers to the 'Finishing off' Review exercises are at the back of this Student's Book. Answers to all other exercises are in the Teacher's Resource.

In addition there are three 'Reward' lessons. These contain games (with a mathematical basis) and are for use when students have completed a period of hard work.

A key feature of the left-hand pages is the tasks. These are the main teaching activity for the lesson, and provide opportunities for students to work singly, in pairs, in groups, or as a whole class. The tasks use the students' own experiences to reinforce the teaching for that particular lesson; many of them are based around everyday life. Each of the tasks is supported by a photocopiable task sheet in the Teacher's Resource; these are designed to ensure the time is spent on maths, not on copying out tables and graphs, and to enable students to build up a body of work that they can be proud of.

The left-hand pages include many discussion points. These are designed to help teachers engage their students in whole-class discussion. Teachers should see the **?** icon as an opportunity and an invitation.

The last part of each lesson is the plenary. The teacher and students discuss what they have been doing and the mathematics involved. This is usually supported by discussion points in the Student's Book, and by quite extensive advice in the Teacher's Resource. The Teacher's Resource also includes lesson objectives, and the plenary is the time to check that these have been met.

The various icons and instructions used in this book are explained overleaf.

The order of the chapters ensures that the subject is developed logically, at each stage building on previous knowledge. The Teacher's Resource includes a scheme of work based on this order. However, teachers are of course free to vary the order to meet their own circumstances and needs.

This series stems from a partnership between Hodder and Stoughton Educational and Mathematics in Education and Industry (MEI).

The authors would like to thank all those who helped in preparing this book, particularly those involved with writing materials for the accompanying Teacher's Resource.

Roger Porkess   2004
Series Editor

How to use this book

 You will have a discussion about this point with your teacher and the rest of the class.

 Use your calculator for this question.

 You are not allowed to use your calculator for this question.

 Your teacher may give you a sheet to write on. This will save time copying out tables and graphs.

 Warning. This is a common mistake. Or, take extra care over this question.

 There is some ICT material in the Teacher's Resource for this work.

This book is a series of double-page spreads. The left-hand page is the teaching page. The right-hand page gives exercise questions, activities or investigations on the topic.

You will also come across the following features.

This is the main activity of the lesson. You are expected to spend quite a lot of time on it. It will help you understand the work. Ask your teacher if you need help.

 Do the right thing!

You are learning something practical here. There are step-by-step instructions to follow.

Contents

1 Co-ordinates

Review

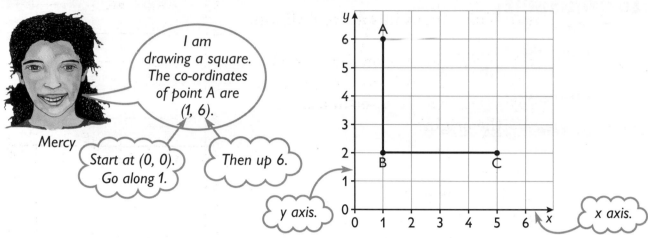

I am drawing a square. The co-ordinates of point A are (1, 6).

Mercy

Start at (0, 0). Go along 1.

Then up 6.

y axis.

x axis.

? **What are the co-ordinates of point C?**

Mercy completes the square with another point.

? **What are its co-ordinates?**

Task

1 On squared paper, draw an *x* axis from 1 to 20 and a *y* axis from 1 to 20.

2 Plot these co-ordinates and join them in order to make 4 different shapes.
   (a) (5, 10) (7, 10) (7, 20) (5, 20) (5, 10)
   (b) (0, 4) (6, 4) (3, 9) (0, 4)
   (c) (10, 13) (13, 11) (16, 13) (16, 17) (13, 19) (10, 17) (10, 13)
   (d) (12, 2) (17, 2) (20, 10) (12, 7) (12, 2)

3 Find out the name of each shape.

4 Draw a **different** shape of your own.

5 Write instructions giving the co-ordinates of your shape.

6 Swap instructions with a friend.

? **The point (0, 0) has a special name. What is it called?**

Exercise

1 Look at this grid.

(a) Which point has an x co-ordinate of 3?

(b) Which point has a y co-ordinate of 2?

(c) Which point is on the x axis?

(d) Which point is on the y axis?

(e) What are the co-ordinates of the origin?

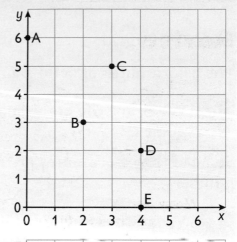

2 Look at this grid.

(a) (i) Write down the co-ordinates of the points L, M, N, P and Q.

(ii) What do you notice?

(b) (i) Write down the co-ordinates of the points R, M, S and T.

(ii) What do you notice?

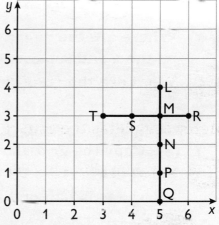

3 Mark and Christina play a game with two dice.
Each of the dice is numbered 1 to 6.
One of them is red and the other is blue.
Each player throws the two dice.

The player wins a point if the numbers on the two dice are the same.

(a) Copy this grid.

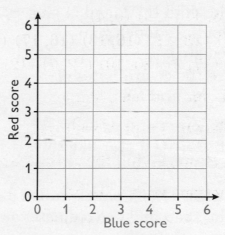

(b) Put crosses on the grid to show all the winning numbers.

Negative co-ordinates

Look at this grid.

The co-ordinates of point B are (2, 2).

? **What are the co-ordinates of point D?**

Some of the co-ordinates are **negative** numbers.

? **What does negative mean?**
What about positive?

? **Where are the negative co-ordinates on the x and y axes?**

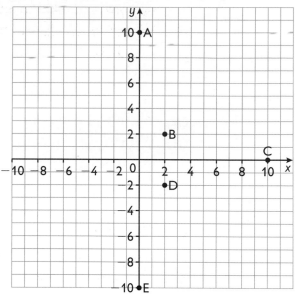

Task

1 (a) Copy the grid above and mark the points A, B, C, D and E. Join them in order.

The shape is half of a 4-pointed star.

(b) Mark 3 new points on the grid and join them to complete the star.

(c) Write down the co-ordinates of the 3 new points.

2 (a) Add the points L, M, and N to your grid. Join L, M, and N and make the lines touch your 4-pointed star.

(b) What are the co-ordinates of points L, M, and N?

3 Mark 9 more points and draw lines to make an **8-pointed** star like this.

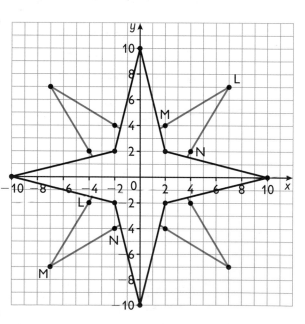

The grid has four parts. Each part is called a **quadrant**.
In the first quadrant, the x and y co-ordinates are always **positive**.

? **Are the x and y co-ordinates positive or negative in the other three quadrants?**

Exercise

1 **(a)** Write down the co-ordinates of points A, B, C and D.

(b) Which point is in the third quadrant?

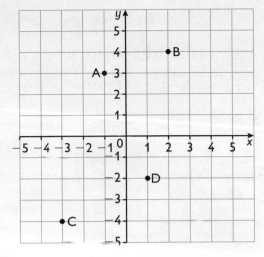

2 **(a)** On squared paper, draw an x axis from -10 to 10 and a y axis from -6 to 4.

(b) Plot these points and join them in order.

$(-10, 1)$ $(6, 1)$ $(7, 3)$ $(9, 3)$ $(10, 1)$ $(10, -1)$ $(9, -3)$ $(7, -3)$ $(6, -1)$
$(-5, -1)$ $(-5, -5)$ $(-6, -5)$ $(-6, -2)$ $(-7, -2)$ $(-7, -3)$
$(-8, -3)$ $(-8, -2)$ $(-9, -2)$ $(-9, -4)$ $(-10, -4)$ $(-10, 1)$

(c) What have you drawn?

3 **(a)** What is the name of this shape?

(b) Write down the co-ordinates of points A, B, C, D, E, F, G and H.

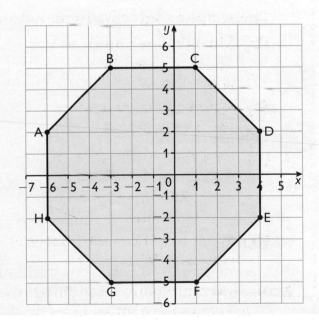

Activity **1** On squared paper, draw x and y axes from -10 to 10.

2 Draw a picture of your own, use all four quadrants of the grid.

3 Write the co-ordinates of the picture in order.
Give them to a friend.

4 Ask your friend to draw your picture.

Using all 4 quadrants

Samir and Michelle are playing a game of **Squares**.
They take turns to mark points on the grid.

Michelle

Samir

The winner is the player with the most squares in
their colour.

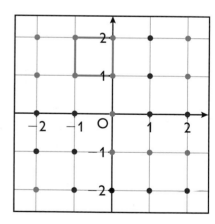

? **What are the co-ordinates of Samir's square?**

? **What other blue squares can you find?**

Task

Play some games of **Squares** with a friend.
Write down the co-ordinates of all the squares in your colour.
Use a larger grid to make the game harder.

Three points of a square have co-ordinates (1, 1), (1, 4) and (−2, 4).

? **What are the co-ordinates of the fourth point?**

*Work out the answer
without using a grid.*

Exercise

1 On this grid, points A, B and C are three points of a rectangle.

(a) What are the co-ordinates of points A, B and C?

(b) What are the co-ordinates of the fourth point of the rectangle?

(c) How long is the rectangle?

(d) How wide is the rectangle?

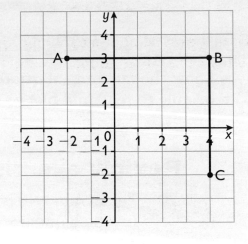

2 Three points of a rectangle are $(-2, 1)$, $(5, 1)$ and $(-2, -2)$. What are the co-ordinates of the fourth point of the rectangle?

Activity

SU

This grid shows part of a pattern. The pattern has two lines of symmetry. The lines of symmetry of the pattern are the *x* axis and the *y* axis.

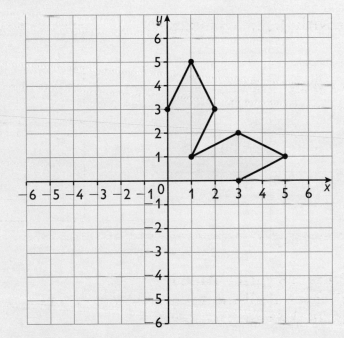

1 Copy the grid and complete the pattern.

2 Write down the co-ordinates of all the points of the pattern in the second quadrant.

3 Do the same for the third and fourth quadrants.

Finishing off

Now that you have finished this chapter you should:

- know the meaning of **quadrant**
- be able to read and plot co-ordinates in all four quadrants.

Review exercise

1 The point (1, 3) is in the first quadrant.
In which quadrants are these points?

$(-3, -6)$ $(5, -10)$ $(-3, 8)$ $(100, 100)$

2nd quadrant	1st quadrant
3rd quadrant	4th quadrant

2 Write down the co-ordinates of the points A, B, C, D, E, F, G, H, J and K.

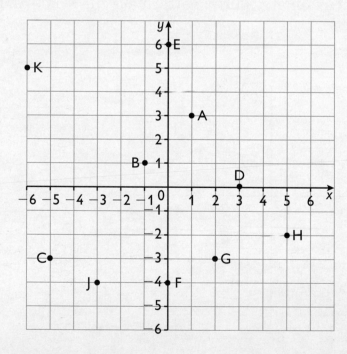

3 **(a)** Draw x and y axes each from -5 to 5.
   (b) Plot the points $(-1, 4)$, $(-2, 2)$, $(1, -2)$ and $(1, 3)$.
   (c) Join the points in order, and join the last point to the first.
   (d) What shape have you drawn?

Activity

Meena and Alan are playing **Find the Fox**.
Meena hides the fox at the point $(-3, 2)$.

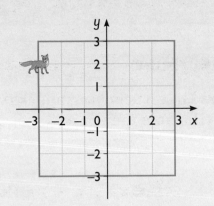

Alan has to guess where the fox is.
He guesses the point $(2, -1)$.
Meena says he is 8 steps away.

5 across + 3 up.

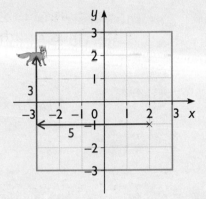

Alan then guesses $(-2, 3)$.

? **Why is $(-2, 3)$ a sensible guess?**

? **How far away is Alan now?**

Alan knows the fox is at either $(-1, 2)$ or $(-3, 2)$.

? **How does he know?**

Alan *Meena*

Play **Find the Fox** with a friend.
Try playing the game on a larger grid.

2 Numbers

Review

Mrs Green is buying snacks for the Year 8 outing.

Mrs Green

I'll have 70 please.

Snacks 80p each

? **You know that $7 \times 8 = 56$.**

How much do the snacks cost in pence? What about in pounds (£)?

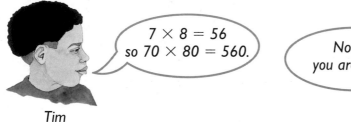

Tim

$7 \times 8 = 56$
so $70 \times 80 = 560$.

No Tim,
you are wrong!

? **Explain why Tim is wrong.**

Task

1 Write down 12 number sentences based on $9 \times 6 = 54$.
For example,

$$9000 \times 6 = 54\,000$$

2 Look at this number web.

On a copy, fill in each of the boxes with one of these.

×2	÷2	×10
÷10	×100	÷100

One has been done for you.

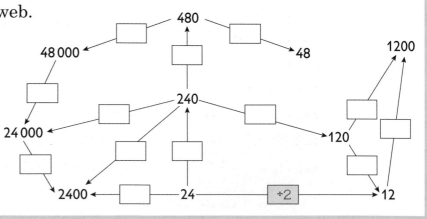

? **Copy and continue these sequences:**
(a) one, ten, hundred, ▮▮▮, ▮▮▮, ▮▮▮.
(b) one, one tenth, one hundredth, ▮▮▮, ▮▮▮, ▮▮▮.

Exercise

1 Look at this abacus.

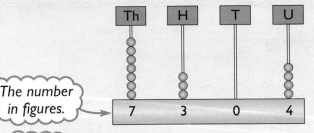

Write the numbers shown by the abacuses below in figures and in words.

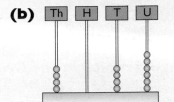

The number in figures. → | 7 | 3 | 0 | 4 |

The number in words. → Seven thousand, three hundred and four

(a) 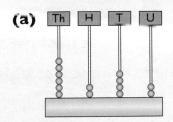   **(b)** Th H T U   **(c)**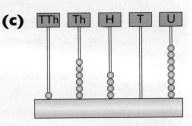

2 Look at these cards.

What is the smallest 3-digit number you can make with these cards?

Jo

*It is **one hundred and three**. What is the largest?*

Karl

Make the smallest and largest 4-, 5- and 6-digit numbers you can from the digit cards. Write them in a copy of this table.

	Smallest	Largest
4-digit number		
5-digit number		
6-digit number		

3 Copy and complete these.

(a) (i) $5.0 \times 10 =$ ▢   **(ii)** $6.5 \times 10 =$ ▢   **(iii)** $7.12 \times 10 =$ ▢

(b) (i) $2.5 \times 100 =$ ▢   **(ii)** $2.03 \times 100 =$ ▢   **(iii)** $21.4 \times 100 =$ ▢

(c) (i) $21 \times 1000 =$ ▢   **(ii)** $2.14 \times 1000 =$ ▢   **(iii)** $25.9 \times 1000 =$ ▢

4 Copy and complete these.

(a) (i) $2310 \div 10 =$ ▢   **(ii)** $2310 \div 100 =$ ▢   **(iii)** $2310 \div 1000 =$ ▢

(b) (i) $231 \div 10 =$ ▢   **(ii)** $231 \div 100 =$ ▢   **(iii)** $231 \div 1000 =$ ▢

(c) (i) $23.1 \div 10 =$ ▢   **(ii)** $23.1 \div 100 =$ ▢   **(iii)** $23.1 \div 1000 =$ ▢

Ordering

FRANK BUSEMANN   (GER)   8351
TOMAS DVORAK   (CZE)   8385
CHRIS HUFFINS   (USA)   8595
DEAN MACEY   (GBR)   8561
ERKI NOOL   (EST)   8641
TOM PAPPAS   (USA)   8425
ROMAN SEBRLE   (CZE)   8606

How close was I to the silver medal?

Chris Huffins

? **Erki Nool won the gold medal in the Sydney Olympic Decathlon. Where did the others come?**

Task

Look at this table.

This column shows the athletes' points after 5 events.

This column shows the points awarded for the 6th event.

| Athlete | After event 5 | | Event 6: 110 m hurdles | | | After event 6 | |
	Points	Position	Time (s)	Points	Position	Points	Position
F Busemann	4361		14.1	954			
T Dvorak	4300		14.3	931			
C Huffins	4554	1st	13.9	986	2nd		
D Macey	4546		14.5	907			
E Nool	4505		14.4	913			
T Pappas	4476		14.1	955			
R Sebrle	4460		13.8	991			

1 Copy the table. Fill in the column showing the athletes' positions after 5 events.

2 Event 6 is the 110 m hurdles.
Fill in the rest of the table.

? **In the hurdles, Frank Busemann's time was actually 14.14 seconds. Tom Pappas' time was 14.13 seconds. Who was the faster? By how much?**

Exercise

This table gives information about British coins.

Value	Weight	Thickness	Diameter
1p	3.6 g	1.6 mm	20.0 mm
2p	7.1 g	2.0 mm	25.9 mm
10p	6.5 g	1.9 mm	24.5 mm
20p	5.0 g	1.7 mm	21.4 mm
50p	8.0 g	1.8 mm	27.3 mm
£1	9.5 g	3.2 mm	22.5 mm
£2	12.0 g	2.5 mm	28.5 mm

1 Look at this number line.
It shows the thickness of the coins in millimetres.

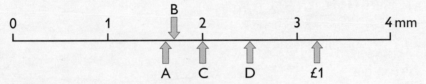

Which coins are at A, B, C and D?

2 List the coins in order of diameter.
Mark them on a copy of this number line.

3 List the coins in order of weight, starting with the lightest.

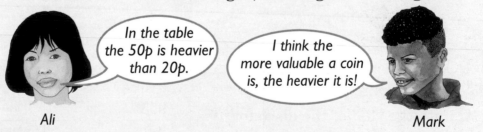

In the table the 50p is heavier than 20p.

Ali

I think the more valuable a coin is, the heavier it is!

Mark

4 Which coins make Mark's statement false?

5 Each of these bags of coins holds £1.
   (a) How heavy is each bag?   **(b)** List the bags in order of weight.

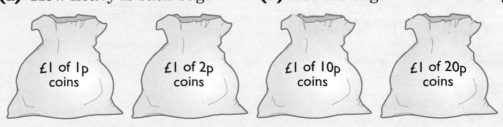

£1 of 1p coins   £1 of 2p coins   £1 of 10p coins   £1 of 20p coins

Rounding

 (a) Round these to the nearest 10.
   (i) 47p   **(ii)** 28p   **(iii)** 85p
(b) Round these to the nearest whole number.
   (i) 44.75   **(ii)** 30.25   **(iii)** 24.50

You are going to use your answers in the task.

Task

Lucy and John are planning a disco in their village hall.

How much do we charge per ticket?

Lucy

We need to work out roughly how much the disco will cost first.

John

FRIDAY NIGHT DISCO
7.30 till 10.30
REFRESHMENTS INCLUDED

Village Hall
Booking Form
£30.25 per evening

Zamba Disco
All the latest music
£44.75
+ £24.50 per hour

Avonford Party Caterers

Beefburgers	85p each	
Crisps	28p per packet	
Coke	47p per can	

Each ticket holder will get a beefburger, a packet of crisps and a can of coke.

1 Estimate the cost of the disco for
   (a) 50   **(b)** 80   **(c)** 100 people.

2 Decide on the cost of one ticket.

Use your rounded figures from above for the costs.

Lucy, to be accurate do not use rounded figures.

John

?

Lucy

 What does Lucy say to John?

Exercise

1 Estimate the positions of the arrows on these number lines.

(a) Give your answer to the nearest 10.

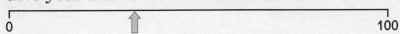

0   100

(b) Give your answer to the nearest 100.

0   1000

(c) Give your answer to the nearest 1000.

0   10 000

2 (a) Mark these numbers on a copy of this number line.

(i) 3.2   (ii) 7.8   (iii) 9.1   (iv) 1.9   (v) 0.2

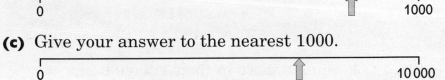

0   1   2   3   4   5   6   7   8   9   10

(b) Round each number to the nearest whole number.

3 Look at the table.
It shows the distances in kilometres between world cities.

Cape Town					
11 852	Hong Kong				
9 672	9 637	London			
13 701	12 121	8 898	Mexico		
10 150	7 148	2 502	10 682	Moscow	
8 684	6 030	14 495	16 247	12 236	Perth

This is the distance from Mexico to Perth.

(a) Make a table like this but round each distance to the nearest 100 km.

(b) Use your new table to give a rough estimate of the distance from London to Perth via Hong Kong.

4 Choose the best answer.

(a) The size of the crowd at an FA Cup final is roughly
    (i) 10 000   (ii) 100 000

(b) You round the number of passengers on a full bus to the nearest
    (i) 10   (ii) 100

(c) You round the number of tomato seeds in a tomato to the nearest
    (i) 10   (ii) 100

(d) You round the population of London to the nearest
    (i) 10 000   (ii) 100 000   (iii) 1 000 000

Using scales

Sophie

The pike weighs 13.9 kg. That's almost 14 kg! It must be a record!

It's not! The UK record for a pike is over 21 kg. It was nearly half as big again!

Pete

? **How many grams is 13.9 kg?**
What does half as big again mean for the size of the record pike?

Look at the scale on the spring balance to the right.

? **What is the maximum weight that can be measured?**

? **What does each small division measure?**

? **What weight is being measured?**

Task

Look at these 3 scales.

1 How are they different?

2 On copies of these scales, mark these record fish in the correct positions to show their weights.

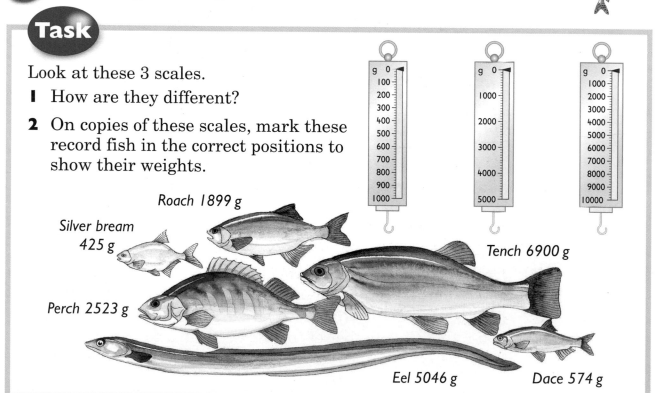

Roach 1899 g

Silver bream 425 g

Perch 2523 g

Tench 6900 g

Eel 5046 g

Dace 574 g

? **The UK record for a minnow is 24 g.**
Where do you place it on this scale?

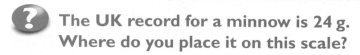

0 g   100 g

Exercise

1 Look at this measuring cylinder.

(a) How much does it hold?

(b) What does one small division measure?

(c) How much liquid is in it?

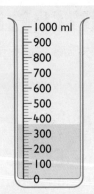

2 How much liquid is in each of these measuring cylinders?

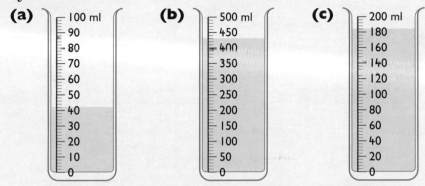

(a)   (b)   (c)

3 This picture shows the dials in Humza's car.

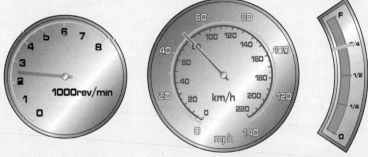

(a) What speed is the car going

(i) in miles per hour   (ii) in kilometres per hour?

(b) What other information is shown on these dials?

4 This is a max–min thermometer. It shows the highest and lowest temperatures each day.

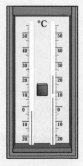

(a) What is the highest temperature recorded?

(b) What is the lowest temperature recorded?

(c) Complete this sentence.

> The difference between the highest and lowest temperature is …

Activity The British record for a mirror carp is 26.77 kg.
Make a poster showing this fish being weighed on a scale.

Finishing off

Now that you have finished this chapter you should be able to:
● multiply and divide numbers mentally by 10, 100 or 1000
● order a set of numbers less than 1 million
● round a number to the nearest 1, 10, 100 or 1000
● take readings from scales.

Review exercise

I Look at these abacus drawings.

(a) 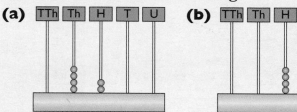 **(b)** 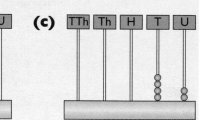 **(c)**

(i) Write each number in figures and words.

(ii) Explain how the pattern changes.

(iii) Add 80 to each abacus number.
Write the new numbers in words.

2 Look at these cards.

Jack

The largest 3-digit number is 976.

Use the digit cards to make

(a) the largest 5-digit number

(b) the smallest number using all of the cards

(c) 6 numbers between sixty thousand and seventy thousand
(list them in order from smallest to largest)

(d) 2 numbers, one 10 times bigger than the other.

3 On a copy of this table, fill in the missing spaces by multiplying or dividing the number by 10, 100 or 1000. In some columns you have to work out what the number is.

×1000					4 200 000
×100	2300		46 100		
×10	230		4610		
Number	23	3000		2750	
÷10	2.3				
÷100	0.23		4.61		
÷1000		3			

4 Estimate the positions of the arrows on this number line, and round the numbers to the nearest 1000.

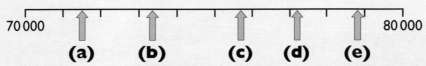

70 000   (a)   (b)   (c)   (d)   (e)   80 000

5 On a copy of this table round these numbers to the nearest 10, 100 and 1000.

Number	Nearest 10	Nearest 100	Nearest 1000
2587	2590	2600	
9449			
16 508			
12 473			
47 900			

6 Look at the thermometer.

(a) What temperature is it showing?

(b) What is the temperature for

   (i) caramel

   (ii) jam?

(c) Between which temperatures is

   (i) yoghurt made

   (ii) milk sterilised?

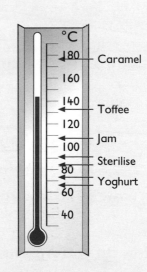

Review

? **What is the difference between these pairs of scissors?**

? **Which pair has an acute angle between the blades?**
Which pair has an obtuse angle between the blades?
Can you open scissor blades to a reflex angle?

Task

1 For each angle below
   (a) **estimate** its size in degrees (write your answer in a copy of the table)
   (b) **measure** its size using a protractor (write your answer in your table).

2 Fill in the third column of your table.

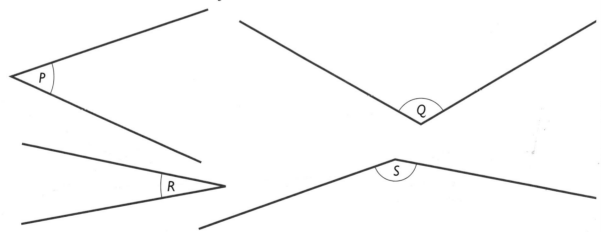

Angle	Estimate	Measurement	Acute/obtuse/reflex?
P			
Q			
R			
S			

? **How good are your estimates?**

? **How do you measure this reflex angle?**

Exercise

1 Draw and label angles of
(a) 40°   (b) 75°   (c) 10°   (d) 135°.

2 Look at these angles.

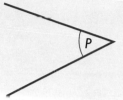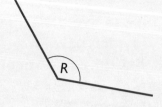

Which angle is
(a) acute   (b) obtuse   (c) reflex?

3 Make an accurate drawing of this reflex angle of 200°.
You have to calculate the smaller angle so you can draw it.

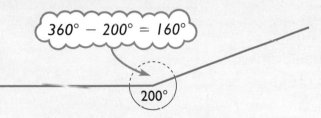

360° − 200° = 160°

200°

4 (a) Measure the four angles
in this diagram.
(b) What do you notice?
(c) Which angles are
(i) acute
(ii) obtuse?

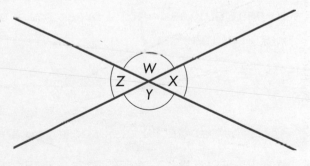

5 Match each red box to the correct blue box.

Obtuse angle

Reflex angle

Acute angle

Smaller than a right angle

Larger than a right angle, smaller than two right angles

Larger than two right angles

Angles on a straight line

Look at your protractor.
50° and 130° are on the same line.
50° + 130° = 180°.

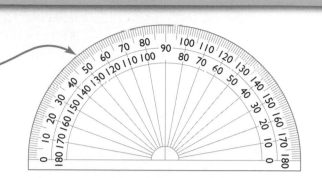

 Choose five other pairs like this.
Add each pair.
What do you notice?

Task

1 Draw a straight line.
2 Draw another line at an angle
   to it like this.

You have made two **angles on a
straight line**.

Acute angle.

3 Measure the acute angle.
4 **Calculate** the obtuse angle.
5 Measure the obtuse angle.

 Are your answers to parts 4 and 5 the same?

Repeat the task with 4 other pairs of angles on a straight line.
For example

 What does the task show you about angles on a straight line?

Look at this diagram.

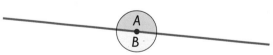

 How many degrees is angle A? How many degrees is angle B?

Angle C is a **whole turn** angle.

Whole turn.

 How many degrees make a whole turn?

Exercise

1 Calculate each lettered angle.

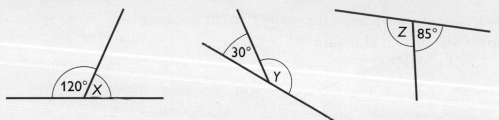

2 A whole turn is 360°.
Calculate the angle between the spokes
on this car wheel.

3 A pipe is bent through 45°.
What is angle *X*?

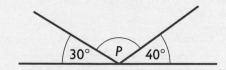

4 Copy these statements and fill in the missing
words or numbers.

   (a) 4 right angles make a ⬚ ⬚ .

   (b) $4 \times 90° = $ ⬚ .

   (c) A whole turn is ⬚ degrees.

5 Calculate the lettered angles.

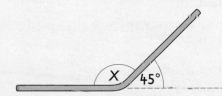

Angles in a triangle

The angles inside a shape are called **interior angles**.

Interior means inside.

? Where does the name **triangle** come from?

Task

1 **(a)** Draw a large triangle on a piece of paper.

  (b) Mark each angle and colour each one a different colour.

  (c) Cut out the triangle.

2 **(a)** Tear each angle out from the triangle.

  (b) Glue the angles next to each other onto another piece of paper.

  Make sure the 'points' are at the same place.

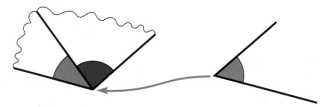

3 Repeat this with 2 different triangles.

? What do you notice?

? The angles in a triangle add up to 180°.
How does the task show you this fact?

? How do you calculate angle X?

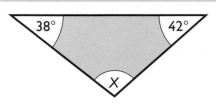

Exercise

1 Calculate each lettered angle.

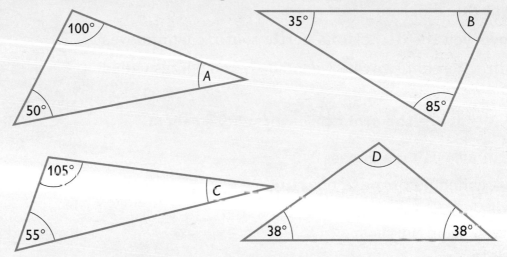

2 Calculate each lettered angle.

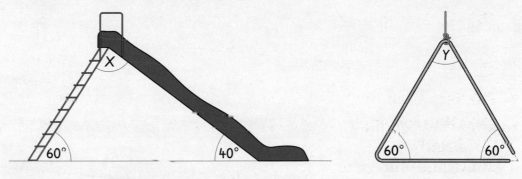

3 (a) Calculate angle *A*.
   (b) Calculate angle *B*.
   (c) Add angle *B* to 70°.
   (d) What do you notice?

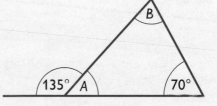

4 Look at the angles in this girder bridge.

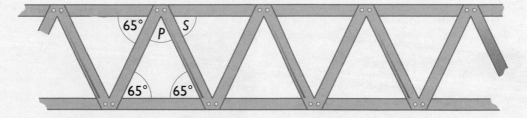

   (a) Calculate angle *P*.
   (b) Calculate angle *S*.

Directions

Look at this diagram.

It shows you the **directions** north, south, east and west.

The direction half-way between north and east is called north-east.

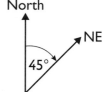

? **What are the other three directions called?**

You can also call north-east 045°.

045° is called a **compass bearing**.

Say 'oh four five degrees'.

A compass bearing is an angle measured clockwise from north.

Task

East is the same as 090°.

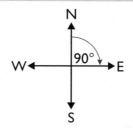

1 Copy and complete this table of directions and compass bearings.

Direction	Compass bearing
North	000°
North-east	045°
East	090°
South-east	
South	
South-west	
West	
North-west	

2 Make an accurate drawing of each of the directions.

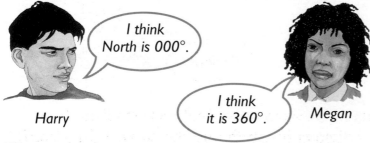

I think North is 000°.

Harry

I think it is 360°.

Megan

? **Can Harry and Megan both be right?**

Exercise

1 This is an aeroplane flight path.
Write down the direction of
each part of the flight, in order.

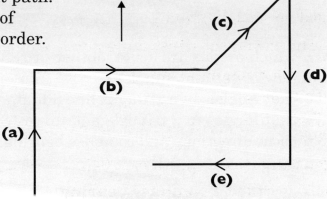

2 The map shows five villages.

(a) You start from Dinton.
In what direction do you drive to

(i) Carnham

(ii) Entor

(iii) Brinton?

(b) What is the direction of Dinton
from Ably?

(c) You drive north-west from Entor.
Which two villages do you pass through?

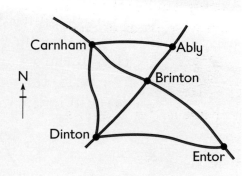

Activity Ask your teacher for a **compass**.
The coloured part of the needle always points north.

1 (a) Write **North** on a piece of card.
Place the card in the north part of the classroom.

(b) Stand facing south.
Turn left through one right angle.
Which way are you facing?

(c) Stand facing south.
Turn right through two right angles.
Which way are you facing?

(d) Stand facing north.
Turn clockwise through 135°.
Which way are you facing?

Clockwise.

2 Work in pairs. Take it in turns to give each other instructions like those
above. Does the person turning always finish facing the correct direction?

Finishing off

Now that you have finished this chapter you should know:

- which angles are acute, obtuse or reflex
- how to estimate angles
- that angles on a straight line add up to 180°
- that angles in a triangle add up to 180°
- about directions and compass bearings.

Review exercise

1 **(a)** Estimate the size of each angle below.
    Write your estimate in a copy of the table.

(b) Measure each angle using a protractor.
    Write the exact size in your table.

(c) Fill in the rest of your table.

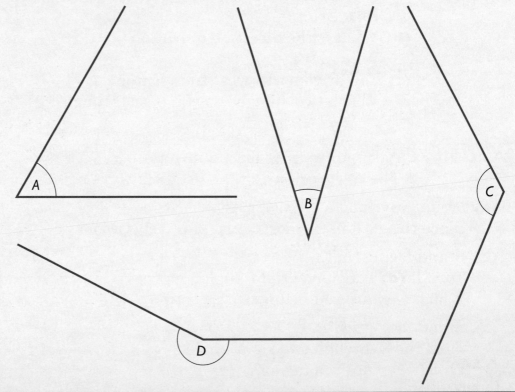

Angle	Estimate	Measurement	Acute/obtuse/reflex?
A			
B			
C			
D			

2 Draw and label angles of
(a) 60° (b) 15° (c) 120° (d) 260°.

3 Calculate each lettered angle.

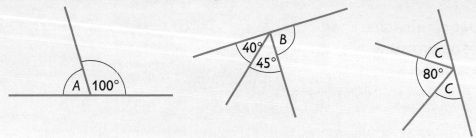

4 Calculate the lettered angles in this crane jib.

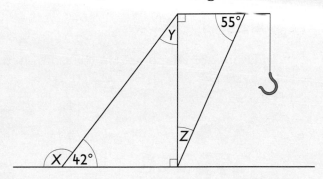

5 This map shows part of the Peak District.

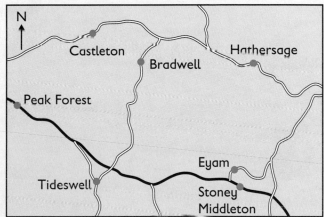

(a) Which village is north of Tideswell?

(b) Which village is west of Hathersage?

(c) Which village is south-west of Castleton?

(d) A glider is over Castleton. It flies on a bearing of 135°. Which 3 other villages does it fly over?

Activity

1 (a) From which direction does the sun rise?
(b) In which direction does the sun set?

2 (a) Fix a pole in the ground.
(b) Find which direction the shadow points
(i) in the morning (ii) at midday
(iii) in the evening.

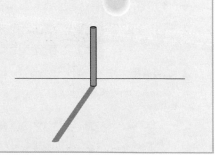

Review

Pete draws a tally chart. It shows the flavours of crisps sold in the tuck shop.

Flavour	Tally	Frequency
Ready salted	ⅢⅢ Ⅱ	12
Cheese and onion	ⅢⅢ ⅢⅢ ⅢⅢ ⅢⅢ ⅢⅢ	
Prawn cocktail	ⅢⅢ Ⅰ	
Salt and vinegar	ⅢⅢ Ⅰ	
	Total	

Pete

 What does ⅢⅢ Ⅰ mean?

 How many packets of crisps are sold?

Pete draws 2 diagrams to illustrate these data.

Flavours of crisps sold in the tuck shop

Pictogram

Flavour	
Ready salted	
Cheese and onion	
Prawn cocktail	
Salt and vinegar	

= 4 packets of crisps

Bar chart

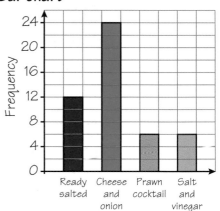

? **Which diagram do you like better? Why?**

Task

Here are the types of drinks sold in the tuck shop.

Cola	Cherryade	Cola	Lemonade	Cola
Cola	Cherryade	Orangeade	Cola	Cherryade
Lemonade	Cola	Orangeade	Cherryade	Cola
Cola	Cola	Lemonade	Cherryade	Cola
Cherryade	Cola	Orangeade	Cola	

1 Use a tally chart to organise these data.
2 Draw **(a)** a pictogram
    (b) a bar chart of these data.
3 Make a poster with your diagrams.

 Use a ⅢⅠ for each drink in your pictogram.

? **How do you find frequency from a bar chart?**

? **Why is it easier to use squared paper for a pictogram?**

Exercise

1 The bar chart shows the coins in Jack's pocket.

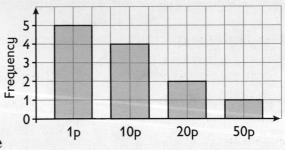

(a) How many 10p coins are there?

(b) Which coin does Jack have most of?

(c) How many coins are there in Jack's pocket?

(d) How much money does Jack have?

2 The pictogram shows the makes of car in a car park.

Make of car	Frequency
BMW	
Ford	
Renault	
Rolls Royce	
Rover	
Peugeot	

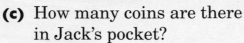 = 2 cars

(a) What does 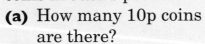 mean?

(b) How many cars are in the car park?

(c) Draw a bar chart to show the same data.

3 Jo delivers newspapers.
Here are the papers she delivers each day.

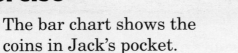

Jo's round

Times	Sun	Sun	Daily Mail	Sun	Sun
Mirror	Telegraph	Sun	Guardian	Mirror	Times
Daily Mail	Guardian	Mirror	Times	Daily Mail	Sun
Mirror	Mirror	Express	Telegraph	Express	Independent

(a) Draw a tally chart to organise Jo's deliveries.

(b) Draw a pictogram to show the newspapers delivered by Jo.

(c) How many papers does Jo deliver?
Add up the frequencies to check this.

Pie charts

Pete draws a pie chart to show the flavours of crisps sold in the tuck shop.

Pie chart to show flavours of crisps sold in the tuck shop

? **What angle is used to show ready salted?**

? **What fraction of the circle is this?**

12 out of 48 can be written as the fraction $\frac{12}{48}$.

? **Cancel this fraction down. What do you notice?**

There are 6 packets of prawn cocktail. This is the fraction $\frac{6}{48}$. It cancels down to $\frac{1}{8}$.

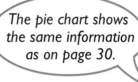

The pie chart shows the same information as on page 30.

Pete

? **What fraction of the circle is coloured pink? What angle is used to show this?**

Task

1 Make a copy and complete this table.

Fraction	$\frac{1}{2}$	$\frac{1}{4}$	$\frac{1}{8}$	$\frac{1}{3}$	$\frac{1}{6}$
Angle on pie chart			45°	120°	

2 (a) Complete this table for the types of drinks sold in the tuck shop.

Drink	Frequency	Fraction	Cancelled fraction	Angle
Cola	12	$\frac{12}{24}$		
Lemonade	6			
Orangeade	3			
Cherryade	3			

(b) Draw a pie chart to show the types of drinks sold in the tuck shop.

? **Can you draw a pie chart using a computer?**

Exercise

1 The pie chart shows how Ali spends her pocket money.

Pocket money

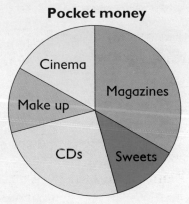

(a) What does Ali spend the largest amount on?

(b) What fraction does Ali spend on CDs?

(c) What fraction does Ali spend on make up?

(d) Ali's pocket money is £4.80 a week. How much does she spend on CDs?

2 Sophie asks her friends where they went for their holidays. She decides to draw a pie chart.

(a) Copy and complete Sophie's table.

Country	Frequency	Fraction	Cancelled fraction	Angle
England	4			
Scotland	8			
France	16			
Spain	4			

(b) Draw a pie chart.

3 Sophie went to Spain. Her best friend Christina went to Scotland. They have drawn pie charts to show the weather on their holidays.

The weather in Spain

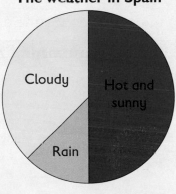

The weather in Scotland

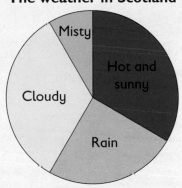

(a) Who had more sunshine?

(b) Who had more rain?

(c) What fraction of the weather in Spain was hot and sunny?

(d) What fraction of the weather in Scotland was hot and sunny?

Averages

There are 3 types of average.

Mr Smith

One is the middle number.

Tim

You find the most popular.

Humza

Michelle

Add the numbers up. Then you divide by how many there are.

? Match the names **mean**, **median** and **mode** with the descriptions.

Task

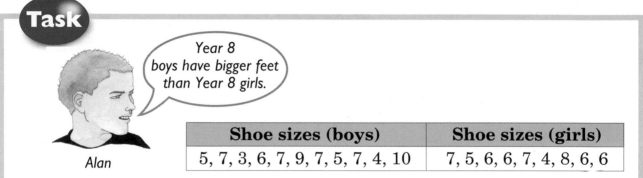

Year 8 boys have bigger feet than Year 8 girls.

Alan

Shoe sizes (boys)	Shoe sizes (girls)
5, 7, 3, 6, 7, 9, 7, 5, 7, 4, 10	7, 5, 6, 6, 7, 4, 8, 6, 6

1 Copy and complete this table to show all the averages.

	Boys	Girls
Mean		
Mode		
Median		

2 Who have the bigger feet, the Year 8 boys or the Year 8 girls.

3 Which type of average did you use to decide?

Find the median of 2, 3, 3, 5, 7, 8.

There isn't a middle number.

The median is between 3 and 5. It is 4.

? Find the median of   5, 6, 6, 7, 9, 10, 12, 15.

Exercise

1 Calculate the mean of these sets of numbers.

(a) 2, 4, 4, 6, 8, 5, 7, 5, 2, 9

(b) 24, 12, 17, 32, 19

2 Find the median of these sets of numbers.

(a) 1, 2, 2, 4, 5, 5, 7, 8, 9, 9, 12

(b) 7, 4, 6, 2, 1, 4, 5

(c) 4, 7, 7, 8, 10, 12, 12, 14 ←

(d) 10, 7, 8, 4, 3, 9 ←

> These sets do not have a middle number.

3 These are the hours of sunshine for Avon Bay one week last August.

7, 12, 6, 12, 10, 8, 12

(a) Find

(i) the mean

(ii) the median and

(iii) the mode for these data.

(b) Do you agree with the poster?

Visit beautiful

Avon Bay

AVERAGE **12** HOURS OF SUNSHINE A DAY

4

> My maths marks are getting better.

Harry

Here are Harry's maths marks.

| Last term | 2 | 6 | 5 | 3 | 7 | 10 | 8 | 6 | 3 | 3 |
| This term | 4 | 5 | 5 | 7 | 8 | 6 | 5 | 7 | 8 | 6 |

(a) Find

(i) the mean

(ii) the median and

(iii) the mode for each term.

(b) Are Harry's marks getting better?

Range

Avonford High School has 2 basketball teams.
The players all have 10 tries to shoot a basket.

The table shows the scores of each player.

Team A	2,	4,	6,	10,	3
Team B	4,	4,	5,	6,	6

Team A are better. They got the highest score.

Christina

Team B are better. Nobody scored fewer than 4.

Samir

Christina works out the **range** for team A.

Range = highest score − Lowest score
Team A   Range = 10 − 2 = 8

Task

Work in pairs for this task.

1 (a) For each team work out

    (i) the mean   **(ii)** the median.

2 (a) Work out the range for team B.
   (b) Look at the ranges.
     How does this help you to choose the better team?

3 Which is the better team? Why?

Outliers

Christina writes down the heights of team B.

Team B
136 cm, 135 cm, 138 cm, 212 cm, 129 cm

This is an **outlier**. It does not fit in with the rest of the data.

 Is the value of the outlier right? Or has Christina made a mistake?

Exercise

1 Find the range of these sets of data.

(a) 12, 15, 23, 10, 19, 27

(b) 101, 142, 99, 125, 109, 150

2 These sets of data all contain an outlier. In each set

(i) find the outlier   (ii) decide if it is a mistake.

(a) The ages of people on a school trip.

10, 11, 11, 12, 32, 14, 12, 11, 13, 13, 12

(b) The midday temperatures in London for a week in December.

2°, 3°, 7°, 24°, 5°, 8°, 0°

(c) The times, in seconds, taken by an athlete to run 100 m.

12.3, 14.2, 11.4, 0.5, 10.9, 11.8

(d) The number of ice-creams sold last week.

12, 15, 39, 15, 11, 16, 8

3 John and Lucy are training for the school swimming team.
These are their practice times, in seconds, for the 50 m breast stroke.

John	47, 55, 49, 40, 59
Lucy	52, 53, 54, 49, 47

(a) Calculate the mean times of both swimmers.

(b) Find the range for both swimmers.

(c) Who do you choose for the swimming team?
Give reasons for your answer.

4 Here are the heights of 5 boys and 5 girls.

Boys	135 cm	160 cm	188 cm	125 cm	171 cm
Girls	128 cm	169 cm	161 cm	138 cm	172 cm

(a) Find the median height of

(i) the boys   (ii) the girls.

(b) Find the range of

(i) the boys' heights   (ii) the girls' heights.

(c) Copy and complete these sentences.

The median height of the boys is about _____ as the girls.

The range of the boys' heights is _____ than the girls'.

Finishing off

Now that you have finished this chapter you should be able to:

- display data
- find the mean, median and mode
- use averages to compare 2 sets of data
- find the range
- recognise outliers.

Review exercise

1   Alan writes down the magazines read by his friends.
Here is Alan's list.

> Pop star, Mizzi, Teen idol, Pop star, Pop star, Pop star, Chat,
> Teen idol, Chat, Mizzi, Teen idol, Pop star, Chat, Chat, Mizzi,
> Chat, Pop star

(a) Make a tally chart for Alan's results.

(b) Draw a bar chart to show the magazines read by Alan's friends.

2

Get more tomatoes with Grow-well!

Karl has 2 tomato plants.
He counts the number of tomatoes he picks each day.

With Grow-well	5, 4, 4, 2, 7, 8, 10
Without Grow-well	3, 5, 3, 5, 6, 9, 3

(a) For each plant find
  (i)   the mean   **(ii)**   the median.

(b) Do you agree with the claim that you get more tomatoes with Grow-well?

(c) Which type of average did you use for your answer in **(b)**?

3 Mercy is going on holiday for 8 days.
This is how she plans to spend her time.
Draw a pie chart to show how she plans to spends her holiday.

Activity	Frequency
Sightseeing	2 days
On the beach	4 days
Shopping	1 day
Walking	1 day

4 These sets of data all contain an outlier. For each one
  (i) identify the outlier
  (ii) decide if it is a mistake (remove it if it is)
  (iii) calculate the range.

(a) Megan's homework marks for Maths.

  10, 8, 10, 9, 3, 8, 9

(b) The weight of 10 bags of crisps.

  30 g, 29 g, 31 g, 29 g, 28 g, 29 g, 31 g, 27 g, 10 g, 30 g

(c) The age of contestants in a skating competition.

  14, 166, 18, 17, 16, 15, 19, 16

5 Here are some daytime temperatures in the resort of Costa Monica.

  21°, 23°, 31°, 29°, 22°, 32°, 22°, 27°, 29°, 25°

(a) Calculate
  (i) the mean and
  (ii) the range of these data.
(b) Make a poster to advertise Costa Monica as a holiday resort.

Activity   **1** Collect some information from your friends, both boys and girls. For example:

  Shoe sizes   Heights   Amount of pocket money

2 Make a poster to show your information.

  Make sure you display your data with a suitable diagram.

3 Calculate at least one average for both boys and girls.
4 Compare the results for boys and girls.

Adding and subtracting decimals

Alan and his family are visiting Grandad in Ireland.

They use Euros in Ireland.

? **How much money is here?**

Task

1 Copy the table. Make up each amount using the fewest notes and coins.

Amount	€100	€50	€20	€10	€5	€2	€1	50c	20c	10c	5c	2c	1c
€46.36	–	–	2	–	1	–	1	–	1	1	1	–	1
€124.88													
€177.33													
€253.07													
€550.77													

2 Look at the prices of food in a café.
Alan's Dad has €30 to buy 5 lunches.
They all want chips with their meals.

(a) Decide what they eat and write an order.

(b) How much does it cost?

(c) How much change is there?

Chips	€1.80
Fish	€4.65
Beef Burger	€1.95
Southern Fried Chicken	€2.80
Double Sausage	€1.70
2 Fried Eggs	€1.50
Super Chicken Fillet	€6.25

? **How can you work out the cost of Alan's order?**

I want 5 beef burgers.

Alan

Exercise

1 Work out these.

(a) £17.78 + £25.46 + £33.02   (b) 12.65 km + 35.45 km

(c) 5.75 ℓ + 7.44 ℓ + 3.18 ℓ   (d) 11.49 m + 21.53 m + 7 m

2 Work out these.

(a) €30.75 − €22.43   (b) 138.23 km − 68.12 km

(c) 20.5 ℓ − 17.6 ℓ   (d) 25 m − 13.5 m

3 Alan's family have their five bags weighed at the airport. They are allowed 110 kg of luggage altogether.

(a) How much overweight is their luggage?

(b) Barbara takes out her CDs. They weigh 2.5 kg. Does their baggage still weigh too much?

4 Alan can take 7 kg of hand luggage onto the aeroplane. His case weighs 485 g. Decide what items he can take and make a list. Check that the total weight is less than 7 kg.

CD player	0.35 kg
10 CDs	0.22 kg each
3 books	0.35 kg each
Present for Grandad	2.75 kg
Present for Granny	1.8 kg
Travel game	0.29 kg
Toilet bag	0.5 kg

Remember!
When adding, decimal points should line up under each other.

5 Write six more number sentences you can work out when you know these.

(a) 3.8 + 6.2 = 10

(b) 0.65 + 0.35 = 1

(c) 0.09 + 0.01 = 0.1

Rounding decimals

Jack and Mark are spinning coins. It is a competition.
Who can make a coin spin longer?

That one spun a long time.

Jack

It was nearly 15 seconds. Your last one was just less than 12 seconds.

Mark

They each spin the coin 5 times.

 Why do they spin the coin 5 times?

Task

Here are their times, in seconds.

Spin	1	2	3	4	5
Mark	11.64	11.75	12.63	10.21	15.12
Rounded time	11.6				
Jack	10.13	7.94	12.31	11.98	14.69
Rounded time					

1 **(a)** List the times for each player in order, starting with the shortest.
   (b) Copy the table of results.
       Round each time to the nearest tenth of a second.
   (c) Who does better?

2 **(a)** Have a coin-spinning competition with 2 friends.
       Spin a coin 5 times each.
       List the times in a table.
   (b) Round your times to the nearest second.

? **How does rounding the times help decide the winner?**

Exercise

1 **(a)** Estimate the positions of the arrows on this number line.

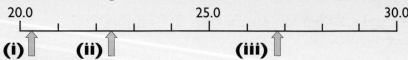

(b) Round each of your answers in part **(a)** to the nearest whole number.

2 **(a)** Estimate the positions of the arrows on this number line.

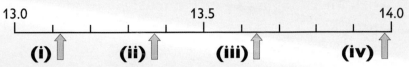

(b) Round each of your answers in part **(a)** to the nearest tenth.

3 Round these numbers to 1 decimal place.
(a) 14.74 **(b)** 19.18 **(c)** 49.97 **(d)** 106.04 **(e)** 28.33

4 Here is Pete's family.

Pete
Height 1.78 m
Weight 90.2 kg

Dad
Height 1.95 m
Weight 90.7 kg

Emily
Height 1.28 m
Weight 28.0 kg

Mum
Height 1.74 m
Weight 83.9 kg

Grandma
Height 1.95 m
Weight 49.5 kg

(a) Who is **(i)** 1.6 m **(ii)** 1.7 m tall to the nearest 0.1 m?
(b) Write the heights in order, shortest first.
(c) Who weighs 90 kg to the nearest kilogram?
(d) Round each person's weight to the nearest kilogram.

Activity

1 Measure your height and your arm span. Are they the same?

2 Find the arm spans and heights of 5 friends. Is Michelle right for your friends?

3 Round the measurements to the nearest 0.1 of a metre. Is Michelle right now?

A person's arm span and height are the same.

Michelle

Multiplying decimals

Elise is from Paris. She is on a day trip to London.
Her lunch cost £5.
She changes this into euros.

Exchange Rate

€1.72 = £1

*£1 is €1.72.
So £10 is €17.20.
Half of that is €8.60.*

Elise

? **Explain Elise's method.**
Does it work for changing £4 into euros?

Task

1 Copy and complete these conversion charts for changing pounds into euros.

£	1	2	3	4	5	6	7	8	9
€	1.72				8.60				

£	10	20	30	40	50	60	70	80	90
€	17.20				86.00				

2 Use the conversion charts to change these amounts into euros.
 (a) £8 **(b)** £60 **(c)** £15 **(d)** £23
 (e) £51 **(f)** £49 **(g)** £76

Alan and Sophie multiply 1.72 by 6.

Alan

```
    1.72
   × 6
  ──────
  10.32
   4  1
```

Sophie

```
  1.72 × 6 =

   1.72
   × 6
  ──────
   0.12   (0.02 × 6)
   4.2    (0.7 × 6)
   6      (1 × 6)
  ──────
  10.32
```

? **Explain their workings.**

Exercise

1 Work out these.
(a) **(i)** 4.38×10 **(ii)** 12.32×10 **(iii)** 0.732×10
(b) **(i)** 2.51×100 **(ii)** 71.55×100 **(iii)** 0.141×100
(c) **(i)** 1.59×1000 **(ii)** 82.11×1000 **(iii)** 0.553×1000

2 **(a)** Multiply these numbers by 20.
     (i) 3.51 **(ii)** 8.35 **(iii)** 10.54
  (b) Multiply the numbers in part **(a)** by 200.

3 Work out these. Write your answers in **(i)** pence **(ii)** pounds.
  (a) 10 rulers at 39p each
  (b) 100 pens at 67p each
  (c) 1000 pencils at 27p each

4 Meena works out the cost of 7 cinema tickets at £4.85 each.
She knows £4.85 = £4 + 80p + 5p
This is her method.

Meena

$\times 7$	£4	80p	5p	
	£28	560p	35p	
	£28 +	£5.60 +	35p =	£33.95

Use Meena's method to multiply these amounts by 7.
  (a) £3.51   **(b)** £8.35   **(c)** £10.54
  (d) £12.88   **(e)** £6.92   **(f)** £11.43

5 Look at these methods for working out £2.46 × 7.

Meena

$\times 7$	£2	40p	6p	
	£14	280p	42p	
	£14 +	£2.80 +	42p =	£17.22

Sophie

£2.46 × 7 =

$$\begin{array}{r} 2.46 \\ \times 7 \\ \hline 42 \end{array}$$

6p × 7 =   42
40p × 7 =   2.80
£2 × 7 =   14.00
Add   17.22
        1

Alan

$$\begin{array}{r} 2.46 \\ \times 7 \\ \hline 17.22 \\ 3 \ 4 \end{array}$$

(a) Use all three methods to multiply these amounts by 7.
     (i) £5.33   **(ii)** £4.62
  (b) Which method do you find easiest?

Dividing decimals

Melissa, Karl and Jack share a Big Fella-Filla.

American Fried Chicken

	3 people	4 people	5 people
Feast-for-friends	£6.90	£8.80	£10.50
Monster Munch	£9.27	£12.24	£15.35
Mammoth Meal	£14.40	£18.80	£21.70
Big Fella-Filla	£17.85	£22.88	£28.15

How much is it each?
Jack is working it out.

*£5 × 3 = £15
so take that off.
That leaves £2.85.
90p × 3 = £2.70
so ...*

Jack

```
        5.9
   3 | 17.85
     -15.00   (£5 × 3)
        2.85
       -2.70   (90p × 3)
```

 What does Jack say next? What does he write next?

Melissa writes:

$$3 \,|\, 17.\,^28\,^15$$
$$5.95$$

 Explain Melissa's working.

Task

Copy and complete this table.
Work out the cost per person of each meal.

	3 people	4 people	5 people
Feast-for-friends			
Monster Munch			
Mammoth Meal			
Big Fella-Filla			

£9.30 ÷ 3 = £3.01

That's wrong.

Karl

Melissa

 Who is right, Karl or Melissa? How can you tell?

Exercise

1 Work out these.

(a) (i) $43 \div 10$ (ii) $12 \div 10$ (iii) $73.5 \div 10$ (iv) $5.3 \div 10$

(b) (i) $151 \div 100$ (ii) $715 \div 100$ (iii) $14.0 \div 100$ (iv) $53 \div 100$

What happens when numbers are divided by 10? Describe it in words.

What happens when numbers are divided by 100?

2 (a) Packs of screws cost 30p.
How many packs can you buy with £3.00?

(b) Oranges cost 25p each.
How many can you buy with £2.75?

3 (a) $£24.20 \div 4$ (b) $£30.18 \div 6$ (c) $£35.25 \div 5$

(d) $£51.10 \div 5$ (e) $£63.91 \div 7$ (f) $£91.08 \div 9$

(g) $£49.04 \div 8$ (h) $£117.70 \div 10$ (i) $£49.26 \div 6$

4 Work out these.

(a) $72.87 \div 7$ (b) $72.48 \div 8$ (c) $65.8 \div 7$

(d) $50.46 \div 6$ (e) $84.69 \div 9$ (f) $71.76 \div 8$

(g) $237.5 \div 100$ (h) $94.77 \div 9$ (i) $127.47 \div 7$

5 Mr Smith owns a hardware shop.

(a) He sells £3.50 worth of 7p tap washers. How many does he sell?

(b) 10 plugs cost £9.90. How much does 1 cost?

(c) A pack of 8 batteries costs £5.20.
How much does each battery cost?

6 Melissa needs some new light bulbs.

Mr Smith sells a pack of 6 light bulbs for £6.30.
The supermarket's bulbs cost £1.20 each?
Which are cheaper? By how much?

Investigation

A length of wood 4.2 m long is cut into pieces 0.6 m long.
How many pieces are there?

4.2 m

0.6 m

Finishing off

Now that you have finished this chapter you should be able to:

- use decimals in calculations and measurements
- compare and order decimal numbers and measures
- round decimals to the nearest tenth or whole number
- add, subtract, multiply and divide decimals.

Review exercise

1 Write these as decimals.
   (a) (i) 43 tenths   **(ii)** 7 tenths   **(iii)** 108 tenths
   (b) (i) 6 hundredths   **(ii)** 37 hundredths   **(iii)** 121 hundredths
   (c) (i) 3 tenths and 7 hundredths
       (ii) 7 units, 4 tenths and 6 hundredths

2 **(a)** Work out how many tenths equal
      (i) 5.2   **(ii)** 7.1   **(iii)** 13.5
   (b) Work out how many hundredths equal
      (i) 0.99   **(ii)** 1.01   **(iii)** 1.1

3 Work out these.
   (a) 0.11 + 6 units   **(b)** 0.11 + 3 tenths
   (c) 0.11 + 7 hundredths   **(d)** 0.11 + 9 tenths

4 Put these measurements in order, starting with the smallest.
   (a) 26.23 kg   27.44 kg   26.61 kg   26.08 kg   27.1 kg
   (b) 13.2 m   13.34 m   13.28 m   13.3 m   13.02 m

5 Work out these.
   (a) £7.39 + £21.25 + £12.30   **(b)** 24.65 m + 17.34 m + 5.08 m
   (c) 29.01 + 7.37 + 16.92   **(d)** £10.71 − £3.46
   (e) 12.35 m − 4.82 m   **(f)** 16.03 − 9.77

6 Subtract these numbers from 10.
   (a) 6.1   **(b)** 4.8   **(c)** 7.3   **(d)** 5.9   **(e)** 8.7

7 Which of the numbers on this number line round to 6?
Which round to 7?

```
├───┬───┬───┬───┬───┬───┬───┬───┬───┬───┬───┬───┬───┬───┬───┤
6.0  6.1  6.2  6.3  6.4  6.5  6.6  6.7  6.8  6.9  7.0  7.1  7.2  7.3  7.4  7.5
```

8 Copy and complete this table of rounded prices.

Price	Nearest 10p	Nearest £1	Nearest £10
£26.72			
£83.44			
£15.45			
£15.55			

9 Jane sells flowers at 25p each.
How much money will she get for

(a) 10 flowers   **(b)** 100 flowers
(c) 50 flowers   **(d)** 1000 flowers?

10 Meena and Alan work out £3.62 × 8.

Meena

£3.62 =	£3 +	60p +	2p	
× 8	£24	480p	16p	
	£24 +	£4.80 +	16p =	£28.96

Alan

```
   3.62
  × 8
 ───────
  28.96
  4 1
```

Use both methods to work out these.

(a) £5.78 × 5   **(b)** £5.78 × 6   **(c)** £5.78 × 7

11 Jack and Melissa work out £7.56 ÷ 6.

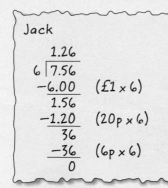

Use both methods to work out these.

(a) £9.48 ÷ 4   **(b)** £14.28 ÷ 6   **(c)** £10.86 ÷ 3

Mrs Green

You all deserve a reward. You can play Loop card challenge.

Loop card challenge

Class 8G play **Loop card challenge** in groups of 6.
Tim shares all 36 cards between his group.
They have 6 cards each.
6 cards show 1000 on the abacus. A player with one of these starts the game.

Turn all your cards face up so you can read them. We can help each other then.

Tim

I don't have a 1000 card. I can't start.

Megan

I do. I start.

Kim

This is Kim's card. She reads it out.

I have

| Th | H | T | U |

Subtract 500 to follow me.

I have 1000. Subtract 500 to follow me.

I think I can go.

Harry

Here are Harry's cards.

A
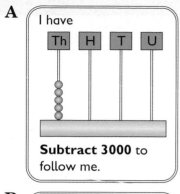
I have

| Th | H | T | U |

Subtract 3000 to follow me.

B
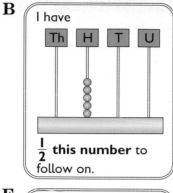
I have

| Th | H | T | U |

$\frac{1}{2}$ **this number** to follow on.

C
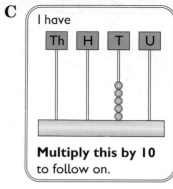
I have

| Th | H | T | U |

Multiply this by 10 to follow on.

D
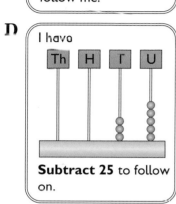
I have

| Th | H | T | U |

Subtract 25 to follow on.

E
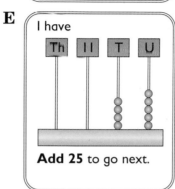
I have

| Th | H | T | U |

Add 25 to go next.

F
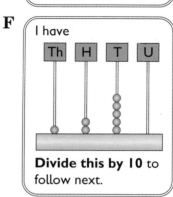
I have

| Th | H | T | U |

Divide this by 10 to follow next.

? **Which card does he put down?**

Lucy thinks she can play next.

? **Here are 3 of her cards. Can she put one down?**

A
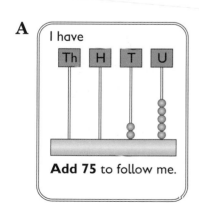
I have

| Th | H | T | U |

Add 75 to follow me.

B
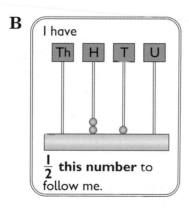
I have

| Th | H | T | U |

$\frac{1}{2}$ **this number** to follow me.

C
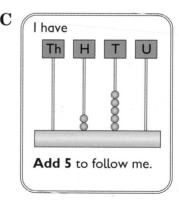
I have

| Th | H | T | U |

Add 5 to follow me.

The winner is the first player with no cards left.

Task

Play **Loop card challenge** with your group.

6 Formulae

Review

Lucy is planning a party.

She uses this formula to work out how many drinks to buy.

> *A rule to work something out.*

| Number of drinks = 3 × number of guests |

 How many drinks does she buy for
    (a) 10   **(b)** 20   **(c)** 30 guests?

Task

> *I need drinks, food and an invitation for each guest.*

Lucy

Lucy uses these formulae to work out how much her party costs.

Drinks:	Food:
Cost (in pence) = 20 × number of drinks.	Cost (in pounds) = 4 × number of guests.

1 How much do **drinks** cost for
    (a) 10 guests   **(b)** 20 guests   **(c)** 30 guests?

2 How much does **food** cost for
    (a) 10 guests   **(b)** 20 guests   **(c)** 30 guests?

3 Copy and complete this formula for the invitations.

| Cost (in pence) = 500 +   × number of cards. |

Party Invitations

£5 for printing
plus
20 p per card

4 How much are the **invitations** for
    (a) 10 guests   **(b)** 20 guests   **(c)** 30 guests?

5 How much does Lucy's party cost for
    (a) 10 guests   **(b)** 20 guests   **(c)** 30 guests?

6 Lucy spends £125 on her party. How many guests does she invite?

 For each guest how much does Lucy spend on
    (a) food   **(b)** drinks?

 Explain the formula for the cost of the invitations.

Exercise

1 Wayne orders some rugby shirts for the school teams.
He works out the cost using this formula.

Cost (£) = 2 + 10 × number of rugby shirts

(a) Work out the cost of
   (i) 5 rugby shirts
   (ii) 10 rugby shirts
   (iii) 15 rugby shirts.

(b) Wayne pays £82. How many shirts does he order?

2 Look at this advert.

(a) Copy and complete this formula.

Cost (£) = 10 × number of ▓▓▓▓
        + ▓▓▓▓ × number of children

(b) How much does it cost for
   (i) 2 adults and 3 children
   (ii) 3 adults and 5 children
   (iii) 1 adult and 4 children?

(c) How many adults and children can go for exactly £50?
There are 6 answers to find.

3 Kim gets a paper round.

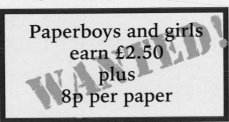

Paperboys and girls
earn £2.50
plus
8p per paper

(a) Copy and complete this formula.

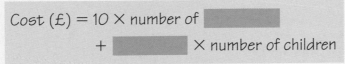

Pay (in pence) = 250 + ▓▓▓▓ × number of papers

(b) How much does Kim earn when she delivers
   (i) 10 papers
   (ii) 20 papers
   (iii) 30 papers?

Using letters

Mark is planning a trip for his youth group.
Mark writes down a formula.

$$C = 20 + 5 \times n$$

SPEEDY COACH TOURS

£20 plus
£5 for each person

 What do C and n stand for in Mark's formula?

Look how Mark works out the cost for 8 people.

$C = 20 + 5 \times n$
$C = 20 + 5 \times 8$
So $C = 20 + 40$
$C = 60$

So the cost for 8 people is £60.

 Explain Mark's working.

 Work out the cost for
(a) 10 people **(b)** 20 people **(c)** 40 people.

Task

1 Look at this advert.
Mark writes down a formula.

$$P = 12 \times a + 10 \times c$$

Avonford Theme Park

Adults £12
Children £10

(a) What do a and c stand for in Mark's formula?
(b) Work out the cost for
(i) 3 adults and 4 children
(ii) 5 adults and 10 children.

2 Work out the value of these when $a = 3$.
(a) $a + 5$ **(b)** $2 \times a$ **(c)** $7 - a$ **(d)** $2 \times a - 2$
(e) $a - 1$ **(f)** $3 \times a + 1$ **(g)** $11 - 2 \times a$ **(h)** $a + a$

Match your answers to these letters and crack the code.

A 1	D 2	E 6	F 7	I 3

L 4	N 5	O 10	S 9	W 8

 Why is it easier to use letters in a formula?

Exercise

1 **(a)** Work out the value of these when $b = 2$.

    (i) $b + 7$ **(ii)** $10 - b$ **(iii)** $12 + b$

  (b) What are the answers to part **(a)** when $b = 3$?

  (c) What are the answers to part **(a)** when $b = 4$?

2 **(a)** Work out the value of these when $c = 2$.

    (i) $2 \times c$ **(ii)** $3 \times c$ **(iii)** $5 \times c$

  (b) What are the answers to part **(a)** when $c = 3$?

  (c) What are the answers to part **(a)** when $c = 4$?

3 Work out the value of $3 \times x + 4 \times y - z$ when

  (a) $x = 2$, $y = 3$ and $z = 4$ **(b)** $x = 4$, $y = 3$ and $z = 0$

  (c) $x = 10$, $y = 5$ and $z = 6$ **(d)** $x = 5$, $y = 3$ and $z = 2$

4 **(a)** Write down how you would work out the cost of

    (i) 3 CDs and 3 DVDs

    (ii) 4 CDs and 3 DVDs.

  (b) Use c for the number of CDs.
Use d for the number of DVDs.
Copy and complete this formula
for the cost of CDs and DVDs.

        MEGA MUSIC

        CDs only £10
DVDs only £12

Cost (£) = 10 × [ ] + [ ] × d

5 Look at this number machine.

| Input | ⟶ | + 4 | ⟶ | Output |

What is the output when

  (a) input = 2   **(b)** input = 8   **(c)** input = n?

6 **(a)** $y = 4$. What is the value of

    (i) $5 \times y$ **(ii)** $y \times 5$.

  (b)

        *$5 \times y$ is
always the same
as $y \times 5$.*

    Humza

Is Humza right?

More use of letters

Alan, Sophie and Pete are at Game World.

I got 3 DVDs and 2 games.

Alan

I got 2 DVDs and 3 games.

Sophie

Game World

DVDs £10
PC Games £20

Sophie writes down a formula for how much she spent.

I spent $\qquad$ $C = 10 \times d + 20 \times g$
I can write this as $\quad C = 10d + 20g$

You don't need the × signs.

? **What do d, g and C stand for?**
What are the values of d, g and C for
(a) Alan $\qquad$ **(b) Sophie?**

*d, g and C are **variables**. This means they stand for numbers which can change.*

Task

1 Pete has £60 to spend at Game World.
How many DVDs and games can he buy?
There are 4 answers to find.

Pete

2 (a) Match these formulae to their signs.
$\quad$ **(i)** $\quad P = 6a + 3c$
$\quad$ **(ii)** $\quad P = 8a + 3c$
$\quad$ **(iii)** $P = 6a + 5c$
$\quad$ **(iv)** $P = 8a + 5c$
(b) What do P, a and c stand for?
(c) Find the value of P in each
$\qquad$ formula in question 2 when
$\qquad$ **(i)** $\quad a = 2$ and $c = 3$
$\qquad$ **(ii)** $\quad a = 4$ and $c = 8$.

A
Avonford Zoo	
Adults	£8
Children	£5

B
Ice World	
Adults	£6
Children	£5

C
Theme Park	
Adults	£8
Children	£3

D
Big Screen	
Adults	£6
Children	£3

a stands for the adults and c stands for the children.

? **Why is Alan wrong?** $\qquad$ **Alan**

Exercise

1 Work out the value of $3a + 2b$ when
  (a) $a = 2$ and $b = 3$
  (b) $a = 4$ and $b = 5$
  (c) $a = 4$ and $b = 1$
  (d) $a = 0$ and $b = 7$.

2 Work out the value of $2p + 3r - s$ when
  (a) $p = 2$, $r = 3$ and $s = 3$
  (b) $p = 5$, $r = 2$ and $s = 4$
  (c) $p = 3$, $r = 2$ and $s = 1$
  (d) $p = 0$, $r = 2$ and $s = 1$.

3 Work out the value of $4d + 3e - 2f$ when
  (a) $d = 2$, $e = 3$ and $f = 4$
  (b) $d = 5$, $e = 3$ and $f = 7$
  (c) $d = 2$, $e = 1$ and $f = 0$
  (d) $d = 2$, $e = 2$ and $f = 7$.

4 **(a)** Copy and complete this formula.

Price (pence) = [   ] $+ 30s$

  (b) What does s stand for?
  (c) Harry goes 2 stops.
      How much is his ticket?
  (d) Jo goes 4 stops.
      How much is her ticket?

Avonford Buses
20p
plus 30p per stop

5 **(a)** Write down how you work out the cost of
    (i) 2 pairs of jeans and 3 T-shirts
    (ii) 3 pairs of jeans and 4 T-shirts.
  (b) Use j for the number of jeans.
     Use t for the number of T-shirts.

Great Value!!
Jeans   £30
T-shirts   £10

Cost (£) = [   ] $+ 10$ [   ]

Copy and complete this formula.
  (c) Work out the cost of 4 pairs of jeans and 3 T-shirts.

Working formulae backwards

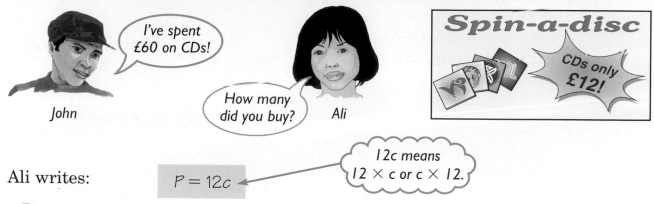

I've spent £60 on CDs!

John

How many did you buy?

Ali

Spin-a-disc

CDs only £12!

Ali writes: $P = 12c$

12c means $12 \times c$ or $c \times 12$.

? **What do c and P stand for?**

Ali works backwards to find how many CDs John bought.

$12 \times c = 60$
$c = 60 \div 12$
$c = 5$

So John bought 5 CDs.

To undo '× by 12' you '÷ by 12'.

? **How do you complete this table?**

To undo	You
×12	÷12
÷12	
+12	
−12	

Task

1 Ali spends £48 on CDs. How many does she buy?

2 Work each formula backwards to find c.

(a) $P = 6c$	$P = 30$	(b) $P = c + 7$	$P = 16$	(c) $P = c \div 2$	$P = 2$
(d) $P = c - 4$	$P = 5$	(e) $P = c + 10$	$P = 20$	(f) $P = c + 7$	$P = 12$
(g) $P = c \div 3$	$P = 3$	(h) $P = 2c$	$P = 12$	(i) $P = 5c$	$P = 10$

Match your answers to the letters to crack the code.

| A 1 | D 2 | E 3 | F 4 | G 5 | L 6 | I 7 | N 8 | O 9 | R 10 | S 11 |

? **Think of a number. Multiply it by 12.**
Now divide your answer by 12. What happens?
Explain how 'undoing' works.

Exercise

1 (a) Copy and complete this formula.

Cost = ☐ n

where n stands for the number of tickets.

DISCO
Tickets £5 each

(b) How much does it cost for
   (i) 5 tickets   **(ii)** 7 tickets   **(iii)** 10 tickets?

(c) How many tickets did each of these people buy?

I spent £15

I spent £45.

I spent £60.

Jo   Karl   Megan

2 (a) Copy and complete this formula.

Cost = b + ☐

Bargain Book Club

Books £1 each
Add £3 p&p
to your order.

(b) What does b stand for?

(c) Work out the cost of
   (i) 6 books
   (ii) 12 books
   (iii) 18 books.

(d) Here are some receipts.
   How many books did each person buy?

(i)

p & p	£3
total	£12

(ii)

p & p	£3
total	£19

(iii)

p & p	£3
total	£7

3 The formula for the area of a rectangle is:

Area = length × width

length

width

Each of these rectangles has an area
of 60 cm². Find the width of each one.

(a) 15 cm
?

(b) 12 cm
?

(c) ?
20 cm

Finishing off

Now that you have finished this chapter you should:

- know what a formula is
- be able to write down a formula using words and letters
- be able to use a formula
- be able to work a formula backwards.

Review exercise

1 Look at this advert.

(a) Copy and complete this formula.

Cost (£) = [ ] + [ ]
× number of [ ]

BOAT HIRE

£4 deposit plus £5 per hour

(b) How much does it cost for
- **(i)** 1 hour
- **(ii)** 2 hours
- **(iii)** 3 hours?

2 Work out the value of $2a + 3b - 4c$ when
(a) $a = 2$, $b = 3$ and $c = 3$ **(b)** $a = 1$, $b = 2$ and $c = 0$
(c) $a = 0$, $b = 4$ and $c = 3$ **(d)** $a = 2$, $b = 3$ and $c = 2$.

3 Mercy is going ice-skating with her parents and 3 cousins.

AVONFORD
ICE RINK

Adults   £5
Children   £3

She uses this formula to work out the cost.

Cost (£) = $5 \times a + 3 \times c$

(a) What do a and c stand for?
(b) How much does it cost for Mercy's party?

4 **(a)** $y = 2$. Work out the value of
   (i) $5 + y$ **(ii)** $y + 5$.
(b) Is $5 + y$ always the same as $y + 5$?

5 Look at this number machine.

Input ⟶ ×3 ⟶ Output

What is the output when
(a) input = 2   **(b)** input = 3   **(c)** input = n?

6 Look at this advert.
(a) Write down how you work out
   the cost of
   (i) 5 bags of crisps and 4 drinks
   (ii) 3 bags of crisps and 7 drinks.
(b) Use c for the number of bags of crisps.
   Use d for the number of drinks.
   Copy and complete this formula.

Crisps 15p per bag
All drinks 50p

Cost (pence) = ▮▮▮ $c + 50$ ▮▮▮

(c) Work out the cost of 4 bags of crisps and 3 drinks.

7 **(a)** Copy and complete this formula.

Cost = ▮▮▮ s

where s stands for the number
of snakes.

JELLY SNAKES 15p EACH

(b) How many snakes did each of these people buy?

I spent 90 p.

I spent £1.20.

I spent 60 p.

Tim

Meena

Mark

Constructing triangles

This shows Pete's model boat. He wants to do a scale drawing of it.

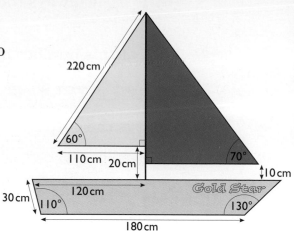

? **What shape are the sails?**

Pete draws the yellow sail.

? **What scale is Pete using?**

? **Describe how Pete draws the sail.**

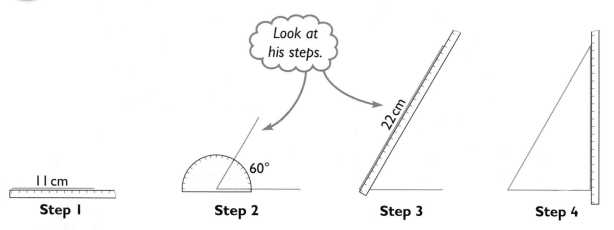

Look at his steps.

11 cm

Step 1

60°

Step 2

22 cm

Step 3

Step 4

Task

1 Use a ruler and a protractor to make your own scale drawing of Pete's model boat.
Use a scale of 1 : 20. Draw the bottom of the boat first.

2 Use your scale drawing to find
(a) the real height of the mast **(b)** the length of the model.

3 Design and colour a logo on the large sail.

? **How do you construct this triangle?**

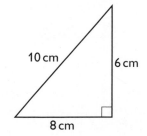

10 cm

6 cm

8 cm

Exercise

1 **(a)** Use a ruler and a protractor to draw these triangles accurately.

(i)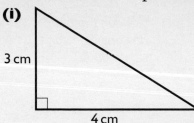

3 cm

4 cm

(ii)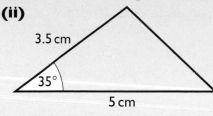

3.5 cm

35°

5 cm

(b) Measure the third side of each triangle.

(c) Measure the other two angles in each triangle.

2 **(a)** Use a ruler and a protractor to draw these triangles accurately.

(i)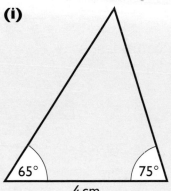

65°   75°

4 cm

(ii)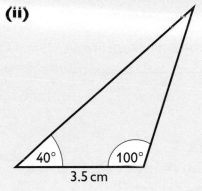

40°   100°

3.5 cm

(b) Measure the third angle in each triangle.

(c) Measure the other two sides in each triangle.

3 Kim's Dad is designing a slide for
the garden.
This is his sketch of the slide.

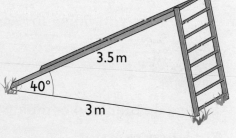

3.5 m

40°

3 m

(a) Use a scale of 1 cm to represent
0.5 metres.
Make an accurate scale drawing
of the side of the slide.

(b) How long must Kim's Dad make the ladder?

Investigation

What happens when you try to draw this triangle?

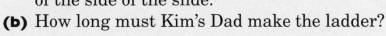

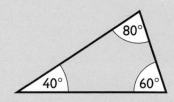

80°

40°   60°

More triangles

Christina is trying to draw this triangle.

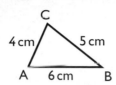

I don't know any angles. I can't do it.

Christina

Do the right thing!

Follow these steps to construct Christina's triangle.

Step 1
Draw a line 6 cm long.

A   6 cm   B

Step 2
Open your compasses 4 cm wide.

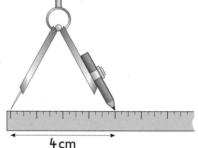

4 cm

Step 3
Put the point of the compasses on Point A and carefully draw part of a circle.

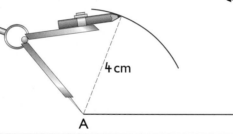

4 cm

A   B

The curve is always 4 cm away from A.

 How do you finish drawing the triangle?

Task

1 Use a ruler and compasses to draw this star.
2 Colour the star.

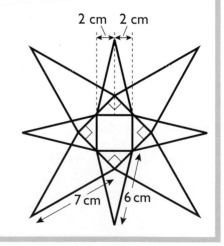

2 cm   2 cm

7 cm   6 cm

 What happens if you try to draw this triangle?

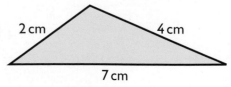

2 cm   4 cm

7 cm

Exercise

Use a ruler and compasses for these questions.

1 Construct these triangles.

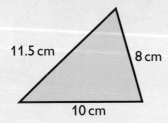

11.5 cm 8 cm 10 cm

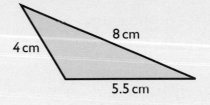

8 cm 4 cm 5.5 cm

2 Melissa is sailing her boat.
Look at this map.
Melissa is at M.

(a) Use a scale of 1 cm to 20 m
to make an accurate copy of
the map.

(b) Measure the angle RML.

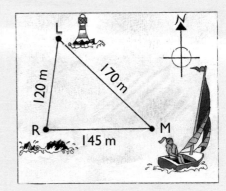

L 120 m 170 m N R 145 m M

3 Construct a triangle with each side 5 cm long.
Measure each angle.
What do you notice?

Activity

1 Design your own star using triangles.

2 Use a ruler and compasses to construct your star.

3 Colour and decorate your star.

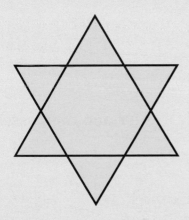

Using a ruler and compasses

Samir has drawn this snake
using triangles.

All the triangles are the same.

Look at one triangle.

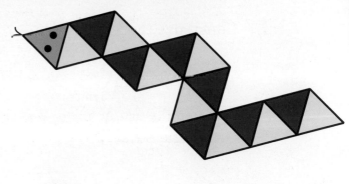

 What is the size of each angle?   **What is the length of each side?**

" Do the right thing!

To construct one triangle using a ruler and compasses.

3 cm

Step 1   Draw a line 3 cm long.

Step 2   Open your compasses 3 cm wide.

*Part of a circle is called an **arc**.*

Step 3   Put the point of the compasses
on one end of the line and draw
an arc.

Step 4   Put the point of the compasses
on the other end of the line and
draw another arc.

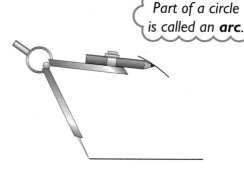

Step 5   Join the ends of the line
to the point where
the arcs cross.

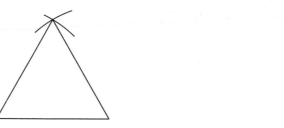

Task

1 Construct a snake, or another animal, using only a ruler and compasses.

2 Decorate and colour your construction.

 **What is the special name for the triangle Samir used in his
snake construction?**

Exercise

1 All these shapes are made from equilateral triangles.

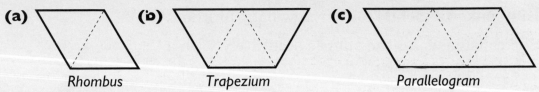

(a)   **(b)**   **(c)**

Rhombus   *Trapezium*   *Parallelogram*

Use a ruler and compasses to construct the shapes accurately.
Make the sides of the equilateral triangles 3 cm.

Investigation

In the task, you constructed angles of 60°.
Look at this picture.
It is a construction of an angle of 90°.

1 Work out how you do it.

2 Try it yourself.

Activity

1 On the computer, use LOGO to construct an equilateral triangle and
a square.

2 Use LOGO to construct a triangle snake like the one in the task.
Or you can construct a crocodile like this one.

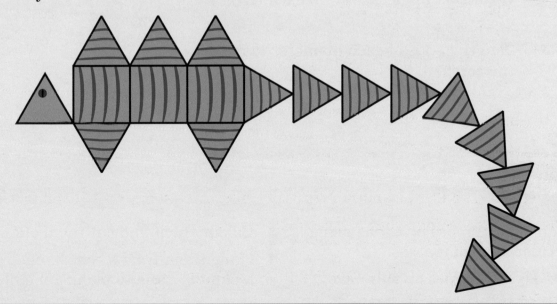

Other shapes

Kim makes a mobile for her new baby brother.

She constructs all the shapes accurately with a ruler and compasses.

She makes this shape.

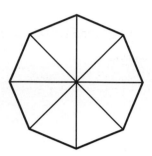

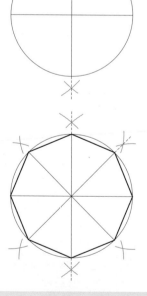

 What is the name of the shape?

To make the shape Kim constructs angles of 90° and 45°.

 Do the right thing!

Step 1	Draw a circle.	
Step 2	Draw a diameter of the circle.	
Step 3	Construct 4 right angles at the centre of the circle.	
Step 4	Construct angles of 45° in each right angle.	
Step 5	Join the ends of each diameter to make the octagon.	

Task

1 Construct 2 more octagons using a ruler and compasses.

2 Stick your shapes on thin card.

3 Colour them and cut them out.

4 Hang them from a coat hanger or a bamboo cane to make a mobile.

Exercise

Construct these shapes.

Triangles

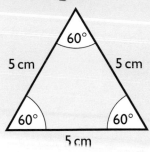
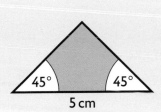
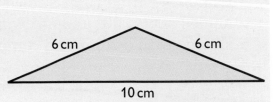

Quadrilaterals

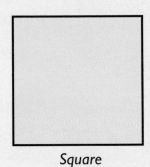

Square

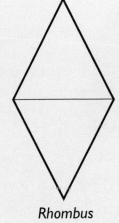

Rhombus

Hexagon

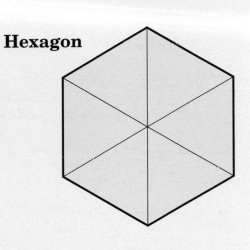

Stars

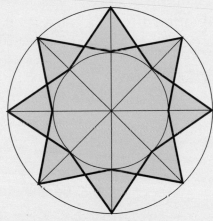

8-pointed star

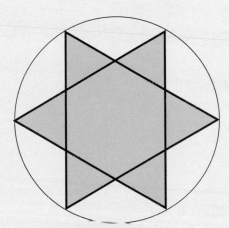

6-pointed star

Finishing off

Now that you have finished this chapter you should be able to make accurate constructions of:

- triangles with a ruler and protractor
- triangles with a ruler and compasses
- angles of 60°, 90° and 45° with a ruler and compasses
- shapes with a ruler and compasses.

Review exercise

1 For each triangle
   (i) make an accurate drawing using a ruler and a protractor
   (ii) measure the other sides and angles.

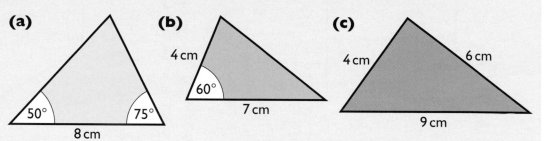

(a) 50° 75° 8 cm

(b) 4 cm 60° 7 cm

(c) 4 cm 6 cm 9 cm

2 Barton is 6 km due north of Avonford.
   Carville is 8 km due east of Avonford.

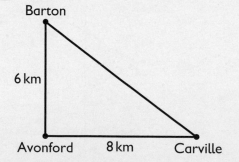

Barton

6 km

Avonford   8 km   Carville

(a) Use a scale of 1 cm to 1 km to make a scale drawing.

Use either a ruler and a protractor or a ruler and compasses.

(b) How far is it from Barton to Carville?

3 Use a ruler and compasses to construct this triangle.

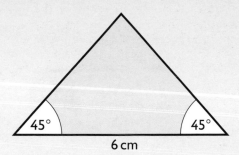

Measure the other sides and the other angle.

Activity

1 On the computer, use LOGO to draw some of the shapes from this chapter.

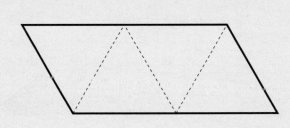

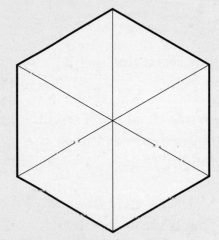

2 Find out how to repeat patterns to make star designs like this one.

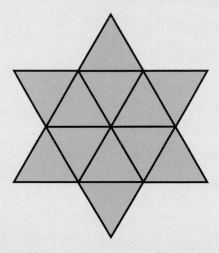

3 Print your work and colour it.

Reading information

Jamila plants a shrub.
She measures its height each year.
Herc is Jamila's record.

Height of shrub

Years after planting	0	1	2	3	4	5	6	7
Height (cm)	20	44	60	68	76	88	92	94

 How tall is the shrub when Jamila plants it?

Task

Jamila draws a line graph.

? **What does each small square represent on the height scale?**

? **In which year does the shrub grow the most?**

Copy and finish the graph.

? **In which year does the shrub grow the least?**

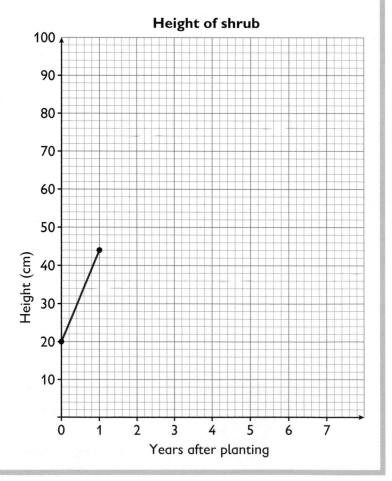

Height of shrub

? **Do you think the shrub will grow much taller?**

Exercise

1 Jamila plants an apple tree. The graph shows its growth.

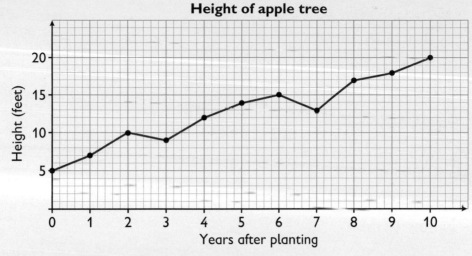

Height of apple tree

(a) How high is the tree when Jamila plants it?

(b) How high is it after 5 years?

(c) When is it 17 feet high?

(d) In which years does she prune it?

(e) In which year does it grow the most?

2 Richard is a stamp dealer.
He records the number of French stamps in stock.

Date	Number of stamps	Date	Number of stamps
1st January	800	1st July	795
1st February	760	1st August	580
1st March	770	1st September	440
1st April	910	1st October	1030
1st May	715	1st November	940
1st June	715	1st December	885

(a) Draw a line graph to show the data.

(b) How many stamps does Richard have at the beginning of the year?

(c) When does he have the fewest stamps?

(d) In which month is the greatest change?

(e) In which month is there no change?

Conversion graphs

Stuart is making a cake.
His mum's recipe is in ounces.

 How does Stuart weigh the ingredients?

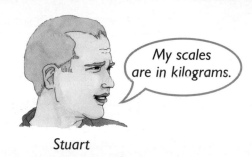

My scales are in kilograms.

Stuart

Task

1 Draw a conversion graph between grams and ounces.
   This is how to do it.

100 g is the same as $3\frac{1}{2}$ oz.

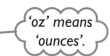 'oz' means 'ounces'.

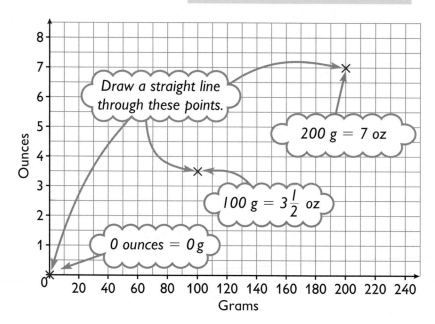

Draw a straight line through these points.

200 g = 7 oz

100 g = $3\frac{1}{2}$ oz

0 ounces = 0 g

 What does each small division on the Grams axis represent?

Almond Fruit Cake
Cooking time: 3 hours.   Temperature: 320 °F.

8 oz butter   3 oz mixed peel
8 oz caster sugar   1 oz preserved ginger
8 oz ground almonds   4 eggs
4 oz plain flour   Pinch of salt
16 oz sultanas   Grated rind 1 orange

2 Use your graph to write this recipe using grams.

 Why is it good to use the extra point '200 g = 7 ounces' to draw the graph?

Exercise

1. Use your conversion graph to convert these weights into ounces.
   (a) 100 g
   (b) 240 g
   (c) 400 g

2. Stuart's oven is marked in Centigrade.
   Here is a temperature conversion graph.

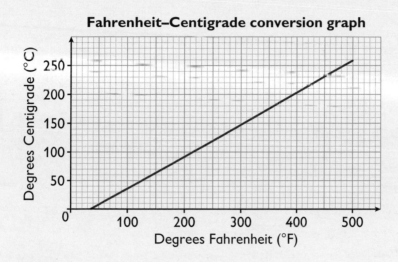

Fahrenheit–Centigrade conversion graph

   (a) What does 1 small square represent on each scale?
   (b) Look at the cake recipe opposite.
       At what Centigrade temperature does Stuart set his oven?
   (c) Copy and complete this table.

Recipe	Fahrenheit	Centigrade
Meringues	260°	
Swiss Roll		200°
Butterfly Cakes	375°	
Rock Cakes		230°
Gingerbread		180°

3. 20 gallons is about the same as 90 litres.
   (a) Draw a conversion graph between gallons and litres.
   (b) A car petrol tank holds 40 litres.
       How many gallons is this?
   (c) Convert 17 gallons into litres.

Travel graphs

Wayne cycles to Andy's house.
This **travel graph** shows his journey.

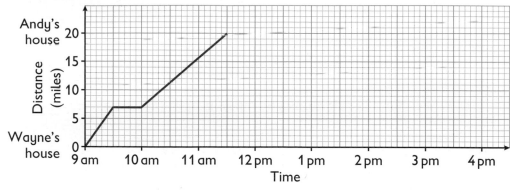

Wayne calls at a shop on the way.

? **How far does Wayne travel to the shop?**
How long does he spend at the shop?
How far is it from Wayne's house to Andy's?

Wayne

Task

1 Wayne stays at Andy's for 2 hours.
Then he cycles straight home.
He arrives home at 3.30 pm.

Copy and complete the travel graph of Wayne's journey.

2 Wayne's Mum drives straight to Andy's
house.
She leaves home at 10.00 am and arrives
at Andy's at 10.30 am.
She stays for 5 hours then drives straight
home.
She arrives home at 4.00 pm.

Add Mum's journey to your graph.

3 (a) At what time does Mum overtake Wayne?
(b) How far are they from their house at this time?

? **Look at the travel graph for Wayne.**
When was he cycling the fastest?
How can you tell?

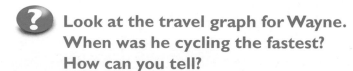

Exercise

1 Mrs Green drives from Mansfield to Glasgow.
Here is a travel graph of her journey.

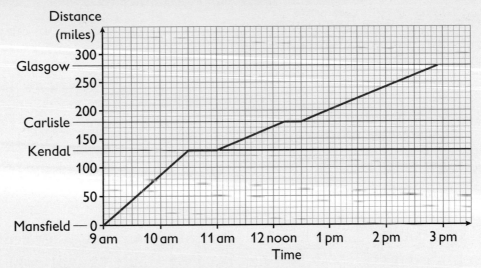

(a) How many stops does Mrs Green make?
(b) How far is it from Mansfield to
    (i) Kendal   **(ii)** Carlisle   **(iii)** Glasgow?
(c) How long does she stop at Kendal?
(d) When does she reach Glasgow?
(e) What does each small square represent on the Time axis?

2 The table below shows Mr Smith's journey to work.

Activity	Minutes after leaving home	Distance from home (miles)
Leaves home	0	0
Arrives at paper shop	16	1
Leaves the paper shop	18	1
Arrives at the tram stop	24	$1\frac{1}{2}$
Gets on the tram	30	$1\frac{1}{2}$
Arrives at work	40	6

(a) Draw a travel graph to show Mr Smith's journey.
(b) During which part of the journey is he travelling fastest?

Finishing off

Now that you have finished this chapter you should be able to:

● draw and read a line graph
● draw and use a conversion graph
● draw and read a travel graph.

Review exercise

1 Lucy records the amount of money she has at the end of each month.

Month	Jan	Feb	Mar	Apr	May	Jun	Jul	Aug	Sep	Oct	Nov	Dec
Amount (£)	50	54	62	48	52	52	61	24	30	33	46	30

(a) Draw a line graph to show Lucy's money.

(b) When does Lucy have most money?

(c) When does Lucy have least money?

(d) In which months does Lucy save money?

(e) Which month shows no change?

(f) How much money does Lucy have at the end of October?

(g) How much does Lucy save in July?

2 One day, £6 is the same as €9.

(a) Draw a conversion graph between pounds and euros.

(b) An ice-cream costs £1.40. How much is it in euros?

(c) Ali buys stamps for €5. How much is this in pounds?

(d) Jo buys a bar of chocolate for 60p. What is the cost in euros?

(e) Tim buys some socks for €7.10. Harry buys the same pair for £5.20. Who paid more?

£6
€9

3 Megan walks and runs to Alan's house.
At the same time Alan sets out to walk from his house to Megan's.

The travel graph shows their journeys.

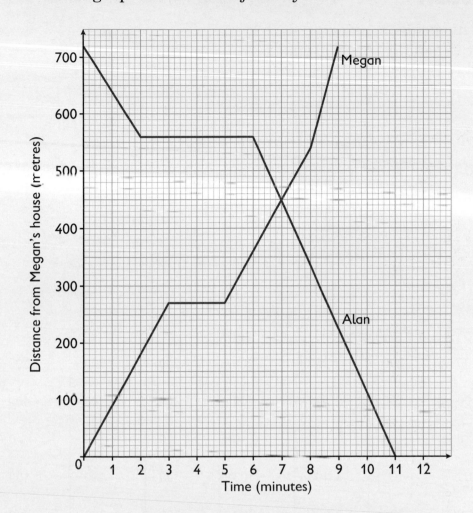

(a) How far is it from Megan's house to Alan's house?
(b) How far has Megan travelled when she stops?
(c) For how long does she stop?
(d) When do they pass each other?
     How far are they from Megan's house?
(e) For how long does Alan stop?
(f) Whose journey takes longer?
(g) When does Megan start running?
     How can you tell?

Addition

Look at this bridge.
The river is usually at −200 cm.
On Monday there is heavy rain.
The river rises 50 cm. *(+50)*

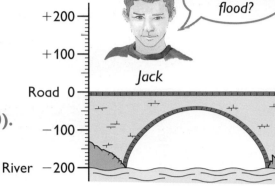

Will the road flood?

Jack

 Explain why (−200) + (+50) = (−150).

On Tuesday the water level falls 10 cm.

(Think of this as −10.)

 Explain why (−150) + (−10) = (−160).

Task

I Copy this diagram.

+200	+200	+200	+200	+200	+200	+200	+200
+100	+100	+100	+100	+100	+100	+100	+100
0	0	0	0	0	0	0	0
−100	−100	−100	−100	−100	−100	−100	−100
−200	−200	−200	−200	−200	−200	−200	−200
Sunday	Monday	Tuesday	Wednesday	Thursday	Friday	Saturday	Sunday

2 Mark the usual level of the river on Sunday's scale.

3 On Monday's scale mark the level of the river after Monday's rain.

4 Do the same for Tuesday.

5 Show the water level on the next 5 days using this information.

6 Join your points to make a graph.

7 Does the road flood?

Wednesday	Heavy rain	Rises 50 cm
Thursday	Sunny	Falls 10 cm
Friday	Heavy rain	Rises 30 cm
Saturday	Heavy rain	Rises 60 cm
Sunday	Heavy rain	Rises 40 cm

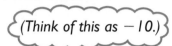

Jack is using a number line to work out (−20) + (+50).
What is the answer?
Explain what Jack does.

Exercise

1 Put these temperatures in order, coldest first.

$0°, \quad -1°, \quad +4°, \quad -5°, \quad -2°, \quad +7°$

2 Here are the depths of some caves in metres.
Put them in order, deepest first.

$-70, \quad -35, \quad +10, \quad -150, \quad -20, \quad 0$

3 Look at this number line.

```
 ─┬───┬───┬───┬───┬───┬───┬───┬───┬───┬─
  -4  -3  -2  -1   0  +1  +2  +3  +4  +5
```

Use a number line to work out these.

(a) $(-5) + (+4)$ **(b)** $(-3) + (+1)$
(c) $(-3) + (+6)$ **(d)** $(-2) + (+2)$
(e) $(-4) + (+7)$ **(f)** $(+4) + (-5)$
(g) $(+1) + (-3)$ **(h)** $(+6) + (-3)$
(i) $(+2) + (-2)$ **(j)** $(+7) + (-4)$

4 Kim delivers newspapers.
She draws a map and calls the main road 0.
The newsagent is at (-6).

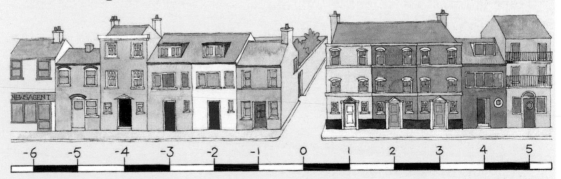

What colour are the doors of these houses she calls at?

(a) At $(-6) + (+2)$.

(b) From **(a)** $+ (+1)$.

(c) From **(b)** $+ (+2)$.

(d) From **(c)** $+ (+3)$.

Subtraction of directed numbers

This photo shows Wookey Hole.
There are many caves here.

The top of the cave is 100 feet above the water.
The water is 70 feet deep.

Cave top	Cave bottom
+100	−70

The cave goes up to 100 feet and down to 70 feet.
So it is 170 feet from top to bottom.

You can write this as

$(+100) - (-70) = 170.$

> *Notice that*
> $-(-70)$ *becomes* $+70.$

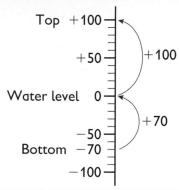

 What is $(+50) - (-20)$?

Task

Here is the start of a cave system.

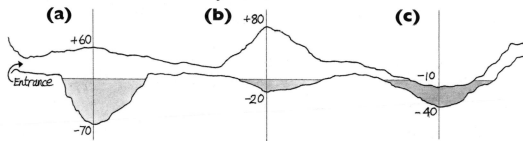

The other caves, in order, are at

	Top	Bottom
(d)	+15	−35
(e)	+25	−15
(f)	+70	−50

1 Draw the complete system on graph paper.
2 Work out the size, from top to bottom, of each cave.
   Write a subtraction for each. The first one is done for you:
   (a) $(+60) - (-70) = 130$

 Work out the following.

(a) $(-4) - (+6)$ **(b)** $(-6) - (+3)$ **(c)** $(+5) - (-3)$ **(d)** $(-4) - (-1)$

Exercise

1 Copy these and continue them.

(a) $3 - 1 =$ ☐   (b) $2 - 1 =$ ☐   (c) $4 - 3 =$ ☐
$\;3 - 2 =$ ☐ $2 - 2 =$ ☐ $4 - 4 =$ ☐
$\;3 - 3 =$ ☐ $2 - 3 =$ ☐ $4 - 5 =$ ☐
$\;3 - 4 =$ ☐ $2 - 4 =$ ☐ $4 - 6 =$ ☐

2 Work out these.

(a) $6 - 7$ (b) $-3 - 1$ (c) $-2 - 3$ (d) $5 - (-2)$
(e) $4 - (-1)$ (f) $6 - (-4)$ (g) $6 - 8$ (h) $0 - 8$
(i) $-5 - 3$ (j) $7 - (-2)$

3 What is the difference between these temperatures?

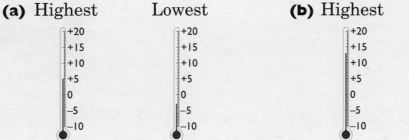

(a) Highest   Lowest   (b) Highest   Lowest

(c) Highest   Lowest   (d) Highest   Lowest
$\;-1$ -4 $+20$ -5

(e) Highest   Lowest   (f) Highest   Lowest
$\;+2$ -6 -3 -10

4 Mrs Green has £150 in her bank account.
She receives a cheque for £50 from the insurance company.
She has a phone bill of £95 to pay.

Mrs Green sorts out her finances on this account sheet.

Credits (+)	Debits (−)	Balance (£)
		150
50		200
	95	☐

(a) Copy the account sheet and fill in the missing balance.
(b) Extend your copy of the account sheet.
     Write these in the correct column.
     ● Payment for dress £85   ● Payment for hairdresser £40
     ● Competition win £100   ● Payment for car repairs £150
     ● Payment for food £25   ● Sale of old car £400
     Work out the balance each time.

Negative numbers on your calculator

Mr Smith

> Work out
> 41 − (−21) on your
> calculators.

Harry and Mercy have different calculators. They have different keys.

Harry

> Look, Mercy.
> I have a +/− button on
> my calculator!

Mercy

> I have a (−)
> button as well as
> a − button.

Harry presses:

4 1 − 2 1 +/− =

Mercy presses:

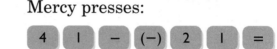
4 1 − (−) 2 1 =

> *This makes the number negative.*

? Look at your calculator. Is it like Harry's or Mercy's?
Work out 41 − (−21) on your calculator.

? How do you do −214 − 202 on your calculator?

Task

Use your calculator to work out the clues below.
Blue squares have negative answers; put only
the numbers in the squares, not the signs.

Across
1 −214 − 202
3 13.5 − 35.5
5 14 − (−68)
7 −15 − (−31) − 89
8 (−2) − (−16)
10 700 − 7 − (−69)

Down
2 (+58) + (−120)
4 −12 − 15
6 −4.3 + 25.3
9 47 − (−2) − 2

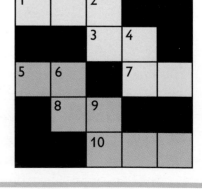

? How many ways can you put −76 − 13 in your calculator and get the
answer −89?

Exercise

1 Use your calculator to work out these.

(a) $12 - 15$	**(b)** $-17 - 19$	**(c)** $63 - 17$
(d) $-33 - (-19)$	**(e)** $23 - (-18)$	**(f)** $-49 - (-73)$
(g) $-132 + 249$	**(h)** $-364 + 157$	**(i)** $186 - 241$
(j) $45.8 - 6.2$	**(k)** $-413.9 + 257.3$	**(l)** $-23.8 - 17.6$
(m) $7 - (-11.6)$	**(n)** $3.6 - 9.2 + 1.8$	**(o)** $6.8 - (-5.9) + 1.2$

2 Work out these.

(a) $5 - 6$ **(b)** $5 + (-6)$ **(c)** $5 - (-6)$ **(d)** $5 + 6$

Which answers are the same?

3 Work out these.

(a) $-3 + 4$ **(b)** $-4 - 3$ **(c)** $4 - 3$ **(d)** $-3 - (-4)$

Which answers are the same?

Activity

(a) Copy the axes onto squared paper.

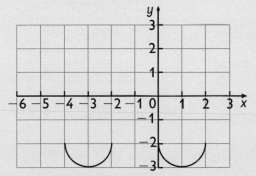

(b) Work out these co-ordinates. The first has been done for you. Write down the x and y co-ordinates in order, as in the third column of this table.

(c) Plot the points and join them in order.
Join the last point to $(0, 1)$.

x co-ordinate		y co-ordinate		(x, y)
$-6 + 6$	$= 0$	$-2 + 3$	$= 1$	$(0 , 1)$
$1 - 5 + 4$	$=$	$-3 + 6$	$=$	$(\ ,\ )$
$-3 + 4$	$=$	$-2 + 5$	$=$	$(\ ,\ )$
$6 - 5$	$=$	$-3 + 4$	$=$	$(\ ,\ )$
$-4 + 6$	$=$	$7 - 6$	$=$	$(\ ,\ )$
$7 - 5$	$=$	$2 - 3$	$=$	$(\ ,\ )$
$-4 + 7$	$=$	$-4 + 3$	$=$	$(\ ,\ )$
$2 - (-1)$	$=$	$-1 - 1$	$=$	$(\ ,\ )$
$4 - 10$	$=$	$-3 + 1$	$=$	$(\ ,\ )$
$-3 - 3$	$=$	$-3 + 3$	$=$	$(\ ,\ )$
$7 - 10$	$=$	$-2 - (-2)$	$=$	$(\ ,\ )$
$-4 - (-1)$	$=$	$-2 - (-3)$	$=$	$(\ ,\ )$
$-3 - 1$	$=$	$-3 - (-4)$	$=$	$(\ ,\ )$
$-2 - 2$	$=$	$1 - (-1)$	$=$	$(\ ,\ )$
$6 - 8$	$=$	$0 - (-2)$	$=$	$(\ ,\ )$
$3 - 5$	$=$	$-3 + 4$	$=$	$(\ ,\ )$

Finishing off

Now that you have finished this chapter you should be able to:

- add and subtract positive and negative numbers
- use negative numbers on a calculator.

Review exercise

1 Write these times in minutes using + or − numbers.
   (a) 2 minutes fast   **(b)** 1 minute slow
   (c) 3 minutes slow   **(d)** 5 minutes fast
   (e) $\frac{1}{4}$ hour fast   **(e)** $\frac{1}{2}$ hour slow

2 Ali's watch loses 3 minutes everyday. She sets it 5 minutes fast.
   (a) Is it fast or slow after 1 day? By how much?
   (b) What about after 2 days?
   (c) And after 3 days?

3 On Monday morning a snail is 7 inches up a wall.
   Every day the snail climbs 3 inches up the wall.
   Every night it slips 1 inch down the wall.
   The wall is 14 inches high.

   What day does the snail reach the top?

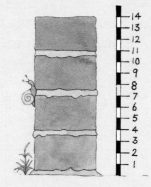

4 Use a number line to work out these.
   (a) $(+3) + (-4)$ **(b)** $(+2) + (-5)$
   (c) $(+2) + (-1)$ **(d)** $(-3) + (-2)$
   (e) $(-4) + (+1)$ **(f)** $(-5) + (-3)$
   (g) $(-6) + (-1)$ **(h)** $(-6) + (+4)$
   (i) $(-4) + (-7)$ **(j)** $(-2) + (+3)$

5 Work out these.
   (a) $(+3) + (-8)$ **(b)** $(-7) + (-11)$
   (c) $(-8) + (-4)$ **(d)** $(-9) + (-2)$
   (e) $(-7) + (+10)$ **(f)** $(+16) + (-14)$
   (g) $(-16) + (+5)$ **(h)** $(-7) + (-12)$
   (i) $(+8) + (-14)$ **(j)** $(+9) + (-17)$

6 Work out these.
(a) $4 - 6$ (b) $7 - 5$ (c) $8 - 11$
(d) $-6 + 5$ (e) $-2 + 7$ (f) $-3 - 1$
(g) $-5 - 9$ (h) $2 - 5$ (i) $-6 + 5$

7 Work out these.
(a) $(+3) - (+6)$ (b) $(+5) - (+8)$ (c) $(+1) - (+9)$
(d) $(-4) - (+3)$ (e) $(-3) - (+2)$ (f) $(-8) - (+5)$
(g) $(+6) - (-3)$ (h) $(+3) - (-4)$ (i) $(-7) - (-1)$

8 Use your calculator to work out these.

(a) $14.4 - 29.7$ (b) $-8 - 11.2$
(c) $117 - (-351)$ (d) $-67.8 - 32.2$
(e) $42.8 - (-22.9)$ (f) $30 + (14.8 - 15.2)$
(g) $-14.1 - (-26.7)$ (h) $-6 - 62.7$

9 Meena and Mark play a game with just one counter on a line.
Meena has the red die. Her score is + (to the right).
Mark has the blue die. His score is − (to the left).
They start at 0.
Here are the first 2 throws.

They are shown on the number line.

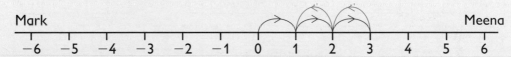

(a) Copy and complete this sum for the first go.

     $0 + 3 =$

(b) Copy and complete this sum for Mark's first go.

     $3 - 2 =$

(c) Write sums to find where the counter is after each of these throws.

(d) If the counter gets to +6, Meena wins.
If the counter gets to −6 Mark wins. Who wins?

Equivalent fractions

? **Explain why Samir is wrong.**

> Half of this
> badge is blue.

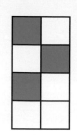

Samir

Task

1 Match these badges to the fractions in the box.

(a)   **(b)**   **(c)**   **(d)** 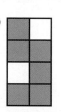 **(e)**   **(f)**

$$\frac{7}{8} \qquad \frac{1}{4} \qquad \frac{3}{4} \qquad \frac{5}{8} \qquad 1 \qquad \frac{1}{2}$$

2 Copy these badges and colour them in.

(a) 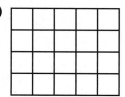 **(b)** 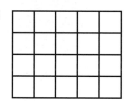 **(c)**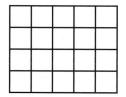

$\frac{1}{4}$ red	$\frac{1}{10}$ red	$\frac{3}{10}$ red
$\frac{2}{5}$ yellow	$\frac{3}{5}$ yellow	$\frac{1}{2}$ yellow
$\frac{3}{10}$ blue	$\frac{3}{20}$ blue	$\frac{1}{5}$ blue

Colour the rest green.

Which has **(i)** the most red
            (ii) the most yellow
            (iii) the most blue
            (iv) the most green?

? **A badge has 18 squares.**
How many squares do you colour for
(a) $\frac{1}{2}$ **(b)** $\frac{1}{3}$ **(c)** $\frac{2}{3}$ **(d)** $\frac{5}{6}$?

? **Copy and complete these.**

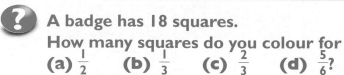

$$\frac{1}{2} = \frac{\blacksquare}{18} \qquad \frac{1}{3} = \frac{\blacksquare}{18} \qquad \frac{2}{3} = \frac{\blacksquare}{18} \qquad \frac{5}{6} = \frac{\blacksquare}{18}$$

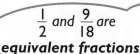

> $\frac{9}{18}$ cancels down to $\frac{1}{2}$.

> $\frac{1}{2}$ and $\frac{9}{18}$ are
> **equivalent fractions.**

Michelle

Exercise

1 Copy and complete these statements.

(a) 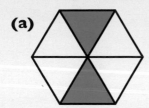 Blue $= \frac{\square}{6} = \frac{1}{\square}$

White $= \frac{\square}{6} = \frac{\square}{\square}$

(b) Red $= \frac{4}{\square} = \frac{1}{\square}$

White $= \frac{\square}{\square} = \frac{\square}{\square}$

2 Look at the fractions below.

$\frac{4}{8}$	$\frac{4}{6}$	$\frac{2}{6}$	$\frac{6}{8}$	$\frac{3}{12}$

Match them to equivalent fractions from the box.

(a) $\frac{1}{4} = \square$ (b) $\frac{1}{3} = \square$ (c) $\frac{1}{2} = \square$

(d) $\frac{2}{3} = \square$ (e) $\frac{3}{4} = \square$

3 Ali walks for 20 minutes.
What fraction of an hour is this?

 1 hour is 60 minutes.

4 The table shows the points scored by the football teams in the Premier League in 2002–3.
(a) How many teams are there?
(b) How many teams scored more than 60 points?
(c) What fraction is this?

Man. United	83	Middlesbrough	49
Arsenal	78	Charlton	49
Newcastle	69	Birmingham	48
Chelsea	67	Fulham	48
Liverpool	64	Leeds	47
Blackburn	60	Aston Villa	45
Everton	59	Bolton	44
Southampton	52	West Ham	42
Man. City	51	West Bromwich	26
Tottenham	50	Sunderland	19

? What simple fraction is the same as your answer to part (c)?

Activity This is part of an Islamic design.

 SU

1 Copy it onto isometric paper.
2 Colour in exactly $\frac{1}{2}$ of it.
Leave the rest white.

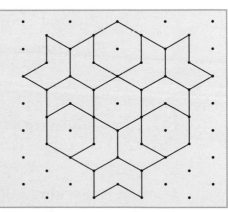

Adding and subtracting fractions

Jack cuts a pizza into 8 equal slices.

? **What fraction is each slice?**

Jack eats a slice and Christina eats 2 slices.

? **What fraction does Jack eat?**
What fraction does Christina eat?
What fraction do Jack and Christina together eat? What fraction is left?

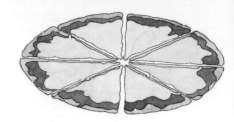

Task

I Another pizza is cut into 12 equal slices.

Jo: *I ate 3 slices.*
Sophie: *I ate 4 slices.*
Humza: *I ate 5 slices.*

(a) Copy the diagram of the pizza.
(b) Colour the pieces each person ate.
Use a different colour for each person.
(c) Copy and complete this table.

Person	Number of slices	Fraction	Cancelled down
Jo	3	$\frac{3}{12}$	$\frac{1}{4}$
Sophie			
Humza			
Jo and Sophie	7	$\frac{7}{12}$	$\frac{7}{12}$
Sophie and Humza		$\frac{9}{12}$	$\frac{\blacksquare}{4}$
Jo and Humza			

2 Another pizza is cut into 15 equal slices.
Jo eats 3 slices. Sophie eats 5 slices. Humza eats the rest.
(a) How many slices does Humza eat?
(b) Make a table like the one in question 1 and complete it.

? **Humza is working out $\frac{3}{10} + \frac{1}{10}$. How does he do it?**

Exercise

1 A packet of Smarties is emptied.

(a) Copy and complete the table.

Colour	Red	Blue	Brown	Yellow	Orange	Green
Number						

(b) What fraction is
   (i) blue   **(ii)** brown   **(iii)** orange
   (iv) red or green   **(v)** blue or yellow   **(vi)** not red?

2 Work out these.

(a) $\dfrac{3}{9} + \dfrac{2}{9} = \dfrac{\blacksquare}{9}$

Why is there no equivalent fraction?

(b) $\dfrac{1}{9} + \dfrac{2}{9} = \dfrac{\blacksquare}{9} = \dfrac{\blacksquare}{3}$

(c) $\dfrac{4}{9} - \dfrac{1}{9} = \dfrac{\blacksquare}{9} = \dfrac{\blacksquare}{3}$

(d) $\dfrac{2}{15} + \dfrac{1}{15} = \dfrac{\blacksquare}{15} = \dfrac{\blacksquare}{5}$

(e) $\dfrac{3}{15} + \dfrac{2}{15} = \dfrac{\blacksquare}{15} = \dfrac{\blacksquare}{3}$

(f) $\dfrac{11}{15} - \dfrac{1}{15} = \dfrac{\blacksquare}{15} = \dfrac{\blacksquare}{3}$

Activity   Look at these fraction sums.
They all have the answer $\dfrac{5}{16}$.

$$\dfrac{1}{16} + \dfrac{4}{16} = \dfrac{5}{16} \qquad \dfrac{12}{16} - \dfrac{7}{16} = \dfrac{5}{16} \qquad \dfrac{1}{16} + \dfrac{2}{16} + \dfrac{2}{16} = \dfrac{5}{16}$$

Write 8 more fraction sums with the answer $\dfrac{5}{16}$.

Multiplying fractions

The price of the DVD player is reduced.

DVD player £240

$\frac{1}{3}$ **off** marked price

? How much do you save?
What is the new price?

? How do you work out the answers?

Task

Copy and complete this table.

Item	Price	Reduction	Saving	New price
Walkman	£20	$\frac{1}{4}$	$\frac{1}{4} \times 20 = £5$	£20 − £5 = £15
Printer	£100	$\frac{3}{10}$		
TV	£250	$\frac{2}{5}$		
CD player	£420	$\frac{1}{3}$		
Camera	£200	$\frac{1}{10}$		
Telephone	£50		£10	
Computer	£800		£200	
Video player		$\frac{1}{2}$	£175	

$\frac{2}{3}$ of 24 means $\frac{2}{3} \times 24$.

Pete and Mark work out $\frac{2}{3} \times 24$.

Divide 24 by 3.
This is 8.
Multiply 8 by 2.

Multiply 24 by 2.
This is 48.
Divide 48 by 3.
This is 16.

Pete

Mark

? Who is right?

Exercise

1 Match the calculations with answers from the box.

| 10 | 36 | 24 | 20 | 40 | 30 | 18 | 15 | 12 | 20 |

(a) $\frac{1}{3} \times 60$ **(b)** $\frac{1}{2} \times 60$

(c) $\frac{2}{3} \times 30$ **(d)** $\frac{2}{5} \times 30$

(e) $\frac{2}{3} \times 60$ **(f)** $\frac{2}{5} \times 60$

(g) $\frac{1}{3} \times 30$ **(h)** $\frac{3}{5} \times 60$

(i) $\frac{3}{5} \times 30$ **(j)** $\frac{1}{2} \times 30$

2 Find the missing numbers.

(a) $\frac{3}{4} \times 16 = \boxed{}$ **(b)** $\frac{1}{\boxed{}} \times 24 = 12$

(c) $\frac{\boxed{}}{5} \times 40 = 24$ **(d)** $\frac{3}{\boxed{}} \times 36 = 27$

(e) $\frac{2}{3} \times \boxed{} = 66$ **(f)** $\frac{5}{7} \times \boxed{} = 35$

3 Look at these fraction multiplications.
They both have the answer 12.

$$\frac{1}{3} \times 36 = 12 \qquad \frac{3}{4} \times 16 = 12$$

Write 8 more fraction multiplications with the answer 12.

4 Calculate the reduced prices.

(a)   **(b)**

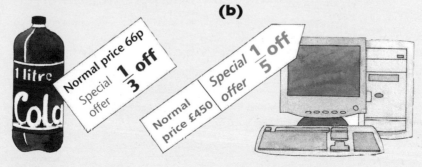

Normal price 66p — Special offer $\frac{1}{3}$ off — 1 litre Cola

Normal price £450 — Special offer $\frac{1}{5}$ off

Activity Design an advert with a price reduction.

Fractions, decimals and percentages

? How many toffees does each person have? Who has the most?

? What fraction is 30%? What fraction is 0.2?

Task

1 Each person has a box of Fruit Jellies.

Meena eats $\frac{1}{2}$ of hers. Look at how much of theirs the others eat.

Henry 10%. Megan 25%. Mercy 0.5. Kim $\frac{1}{4}$. Andy 0.1.

(a) How many sweets does each person eat?

(b) Which people eat the same number as each other?

2 Each person also has a tube of Chocolate Drops.

Meena eats $\frac{2}{5}$ of hers. The others eat these amounts of theirs.

Harry 75%. Megan 20%. Mercy 0.2. Kim $\frac{3}{4}$. Andy 0.4.

(a) How many sweets does each person eat?

(b) Which people eat the same numbers this time?

? What are the missing numbers from this table?

Fraction	Decimal	Percentage
$\frac{1}{2}$		50%
$\frac{1}{4}$		
		10%
	0.75	
	0.4	
$\frac{1}{5}$		

Exercise

 1 Here are some cards.
Copy them and cut them out.

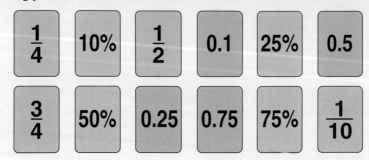

Match them.

 2 Copy these circles and colour them in.
What fraction is green in each circle?

(a)

$\frac{1}{2}$

0.25

the rest

(b)

50%

$\frac{1}{3}$

the rest

(c)

0.3

20%

$\frac{1}{5}$

the rest

(d)

25%

0.5

$\frac{1}{8}$

the rest

 3 Copy and complete this table.

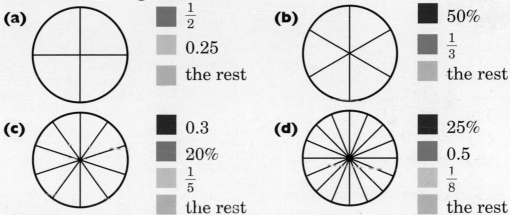

Fraction	Decimal	Percentage
$\frac{1}{10}$		
	0.2	
	0.25	
		60%
$\frac{3}{4}$		
		80%

Activity

 1 Copy the circle.

2 Colour it in three colours.

3 How much is each colour

    (a) as a fraction   **(b)** as a decimal

    (c) as a percentage?

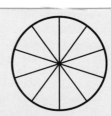

Finishing off

Now that you have finished this chapter you should be able to:

- simplify fractions by cancelling
- add fractions
- multiply fractions
- match fractions, decimals and percentages.

Review exercise

1 Look at these fractions.

$$\frac{5}{15} \qquad \frac{6}{10} \qquad \frac{6}{9} \qquad \frac{10}{15} \qquad \frac{5}{10}$$

Match them to their equivalent fractions.

(a) $\frac{1}{2} = \boxed{}$ **(b)** $\frac{2}{3} = \boxed{} = \boxed{}$ **(c)** $\frac{1}{3} = \boxed{}$ **(d)** $\frac{3}{5} = \boxed{}$

2 Copy and complete these.

(a) $\frac{1}{8} + \frac{3}{8} = \frac{\boxed{}}{8} = \frac{\boxed{}}{2}$

(b) $\frac{5}{12} + \frac{1}{12} = \frac{\boxed{}}{12} = \frac{\boxed{}}{2}$

(c) $\frac{1}{8} + \frac{5}{8} = \frac{\boxed{}}{8} = \frac{\boxed{}}{4}$

(d) $\frac{7}{12} + \frac{1}{12} = \frac{\boxed{}}{12} = \frac{\boxed{}}{3}$

(e) $\frac{5}{9} + \frac{2}{9} = \frac{\boxed{}}{9}$

3 All these clothes are reduced by 20%.

(a)　　　　　**(b)**　　　　　**(c)**

WAS **£35**

WAS **£40**

WAS **£15**

For each one
(i) how much do you save
(ii) what is the new price?

SU

4 Copy and complete this table.

Fraction	Decimal	Percentage
$\frac{13}{100}$		
		57%
	0.33	

SU

5 Look at the questions in this grid.
Some of the answers are right and some are wrong.

(a) Copy the grid and colour the squares with correct statements.

$\frac{3}{8} = \frac{1}{2}$	$\frac{1}{2} \times 50 = 25$	$\frac{1}{2} = 0.2$	$\frac{6}{12} = \frac{1}{2}$
$\frac{3}{4} = 75\%$	$\frac{1}{5} + \frac{2}{5} = \frac{3}{10}$	$\frac{2}{3} \times 15 = 10$	$\frac{1}{12} + \frac{2}{12} = \frac{3}{12} = \frac{1}{3}$
$\frac{2}{5} \times 10 = 2$	$\frac{6}{8} = \frac{3}{4}$	$\frac{6}{9} = \frac{1}{3}$	$\frac{1}{4} = 0.25$
$\frac{2}{11} + \frac{5}{11} = \frac{7}{11}$	$\frac{1}{10} = 1\%$	$\frac{3}{10} + \frac{1}{10} = \frac{4}{10} = \frac{2}{5}$	$\frac{3}{4} \times 12 = 8$

(b) What fraction of the grid have you coloured?

Activity Work with a friend to solve this puzzle.

Half of Melissa's sweets were red.
Wayne had 12 sweets.
A third of Wayne's sweets were red.
He gave half of his red sweets to Melissa.
She now has 11 red sweets.
How many sweets does Melissa now have altogether?

Metric units

? **What does 3.5 kg mean?**
How many grams are there in 3.5 kg?

? **How many centimetres are there in 1.6 m?**

? **What does ml stand for?**

? **What do centi, milli and kilo mean?**

I'm 1.6 m tall.

Mercy

Task

Play a game of **Estimation** with a friend.
Here are the rules.
1 Choose 10 objects to measure in your classroom.
2 Estimate the length or weight (mass) of each object.

Object	Lucy	John	Actual measurement
Height of table	60 cm	0.5 m	58 cm
Mass of textbook	0.3 kg	350 g	320 g
Length of pencil	12.5 cm	120 mm	12.2 cm

Use metric units.

Record your estimates in a table like this.
3 Measure the length or weight of each object.
4 The person with the closest estimate wins a point.
5 The person with the most points wins!

? **How do you decide who has the closest estimate?**

? **Who is winning Lucy and John's game of Estimation so far?**

? **What other units are there for measuring lengths and weights?**

Exercise

1. Match together cards which show the same amount.

   | 2.3 m | 23 cm | 2.3 cm | 2300 m | 2300 mm |

   | 230 mm | 2.3 km | 230 cm | 23 mm |

2. Copy and complete these conversions.
   - (a) (i) 1 cm = ▢ mm   (ii) 1 m = ▢ cm
   - (iii) 1 m = ▢ mm   (iv) 1 km = ▢ m
   - (b) (i) 1 kg = ▢ g   (ii) 1 g = ▢ mg
   - (c) (i) 1 ℓ = ▢ cℓ   (ii) 1 ℓ = ▢ mℓ

3. Change these measurements into millimetres.
   - (a) 3 m   (b) 0.5 m   (c) 3.5 m
   - (d) 3 cm   (e) 200 cm   (f) 203 cm

4. Change these measurements into centimetres.
   - (a) 2 m   (b) 0.5 m   (c) 2.5 m
   - (d) 20 mm   (e) 25 mm   (f) 33 mm

5. Change these measurements into metres.
   - (a) 300 cm   (b) 60 cm   (c) 3 km
   - (d) 0.5 km   (e) 2.5 km   (f) 2000 mm

6. Ali is baking some flapjacks.

I have 1 kg of oats and $\frac{1}{4}$ litre of syrup.

Ali

25 flapjacks need
250 g of oats
50 ml of syrup

How many flapjacks can she make?

Imperial units

Mark

Height: 5 feet 4 inches
Weight: $7\frac{1}{2}$ stone

I'm taller and lighter than you!

Jo

Height: 63 inches
Weight: 100 lb

'lb' means 'pounds'.

? **Is Jo right?**

Task

Put these people in order for
(a) height **(b)** weight.

I'm 67 inches tall and weigh 108 lb.

Lucy

I'm 5'8" and 11 stone 2 lb.

Harry

I'm 6'2" and 170 lb.

Mr Jones

I'm 5 foot 9 inches and $8\frac{1}{2}$ stone.

Megan

I'm 70 inches and twelve stone.

Mr Smith

? **What are the missing numbers in this table?**

Length	Weight
____ inches = 1 foot	____ ounces = 1 pound
____ feet = 1 yard	14 pounds = 1 stone
____ yards = 1 mile	____ stones = 1 ton

? **Complete these conversions.**
(a) 1 mile = ____ feet
(b) 1 ton = ____ pounds

Exercise

1 Copy and complete this table.

Name	Height in feet (') and inches (")	Height in inches	Weight in stones (st) and pounds (lb)	Weight in pounds
Lucy		67		108
Harry	5' 8"		11 st 2 lb	
Mr Jones	6' 2"			170
Megan	5' 9"		$10\frac{1}{2}$ st = 10 st [ ] lb	
Mr Smith		70	12 st	

2 **(a)** Copy and complete this number machine.

Number of pounds ⟶ × [ ] ⟶ Number of ounces

(b) Change these measurements to ounces.
   (i) 2 lb   **(ii)** 5 lb   **(iii)** 12 lb

3 **(a)** Copy and complete this number machine.

Number of ounces ⟶ [ ] ⟶ Number of pounds

(b) Change these measurements to pounds.
   (i) 64 oz   **(ii)** 160 oz   **(iii)** 48 oz

oz stands for ounces.

4 Draw number machines for converting these.
   (a) feet to yards
   (b) yards to feet

5 Karl's dog eats $1\frac{1}{2}$ lb of meat a day.
   (a) How many ounces is this?
   (b) How many pounds does the dog eat in a week?

Activity   Play the **Estimation** game using imperial measurements.
See page 98 for the rules.

Conversions

Kim is making a cake.

My scales only measure in grams and kilograms!

Kim

Fruit Cake
_____
1 lb flour
6 oz butter
6 oz sugar
8 oz sultanas
4 oz cherries
Use an 8" cake tin

1 oz ≈ 28 g
2.2 lb ≈ 1 kg

? **Convert the following to pounds.**

   (a) 2 kg   **(b)** 5 kg   **(c)** 8 kg

Task

1 How many grams of these does Kim need?

   (a) butter   **(b)** sultanas   **(c)** cherries

2 (a) How many ounces are there in a pound?

   (b) How many grams of flour does Kim need?

3 Look at your ruler. Copy and complete this conversion.

   1 inch ≈   cm

? **What is an 8" cake tin?**

4 How many centimetres should Kim's cake tin be?

5 Kim has these ingredients.

How much of each ingredient does she have left over?

? **What does the symbol ≈ mean?**

Exercise

1 Convert these measurements to grams.

    (a) 6 oz   **(b)** 10 oz

    (c) 1 lb 4 oz   **(d)** 2 lb

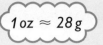

1 oz ≈ 28 g

2 Jack is on holiday in France.
He knows that 8 kilometres ≈ 5 miles.

    (a) How far is 80 km in miles?

    (b) How far is 800 km in miles?

    (c) How far is 400 km in miles?

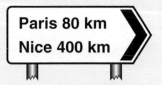

Paris 80 km
Nice 400 km

3 Convert these measurements to centimetres.

    (a) 2 inches   **(b)** 10 inches

    (c) 20 inches   **(d)** 25 inches

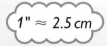

1" ≈ 2.5 cm

4 Sophie is planning a party.
She buys 40 litres of lemonade.

Orange Crush
Mix 4 pints of lemonade with
1 pint of orange juice

5 litres ≈ 9 pints

    (a) How many pints of lemonade does Sophie have?

    (b) How many pints of orange juice does Sophie need?

    (c) How many litres of orange juice does Sophie need?

5 Pete is building a fence around his garden.

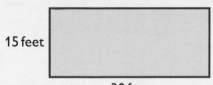

15 feet

30 feet

    (a) How many feet of fencing does Pete need?

    (b) **(i)** How many inches are there in 1 foot?

         (ii) How many centimetres are there in 1 foot?

        (iii) How many centimetres are there in 10 feet?

        (iv) How many metres are there in 10 feet?

    (c) How many metres of fencing does Pete need?

Finishing off

Now that you have finished this chapter you should be able to:

- understand metric and imperial measures
- convert between metric units of length, weight and volume
- convert between imperial units of length and weight
- convert between metric and imperial units.

Review exercise

1 Put each of these words in the table.

> pints centimetres miles stones kilograms
> millimetres litres grams feet metres yards
> pounds inches ounces millilitres kilometres

	Metric	Imperial
Length		
Weight (mass)		
Capacity (volume)		

2 **(a)** **(i)** How many ounces (oz) are there in one pound (lb)?

(ii) How many pounds are there in one stone?

(b) Put these weights in order, highest first.

> 12 lb   176 oz $1\frac{1}{2}$ stones
>
> 10 lb 13 oz   180 oz   1 stone 4 lb

3

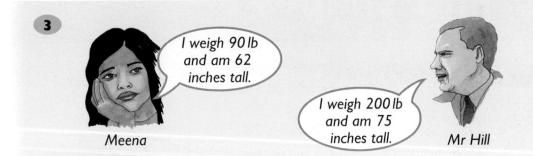

Meena · Mr Hill

I weigh 90 lb and am 62 inches tall.

I weigh 200 lb and am 75 inches tall.

(a) Work out the weight of each person in stones and pounds.
(b) Work out the height of each person in feet and inches.

4 Convert these measurements to miles.

(a) 16 km   **(b)** 32 km
(c) 40 km   **(d)** 56 km

8 kilometres ≈ 5 miles

5 Convert these measurements to kilometres.

(a) 15 miles   **(b)** 30 miles
(c) 100 miles   **(d)** 200 miles

6 Match each of these to one of the weights below.

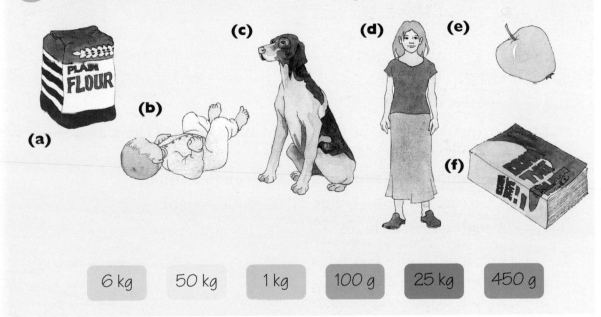

6 kg   50 kg   1 kg   100 g   25 kg   450 g

Activity Design a poster about units.
Choose one of these titles.

1 How to convert between metric units.
2 How to convert between imperial units.
3 How to convert between metric and imperial units.

Review

? **Which triangle is the odd one out?**

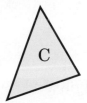
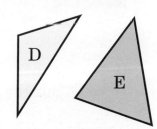

Task

1 You can classify triangles by looking at the length of their sides.

(a) Match each type to its correct description.

Scalene triangle	3 equal sides
Equilateral triangle	2 equal sides
Isosceles triangle	All sides different

(b) Draw 3 of each type of triangle and measure their angles.

(c) Complete these statements.

An equilateral triangle has ☐ angles equal.

An isosceles triangle has ☐ angles equal.

A scalene triangle has ☐ angles equal.

2 You can also classify triangles
by looking at their angles.
Match each type to its diagram.

Obtuse-angled

Right-angled

Acute-angled

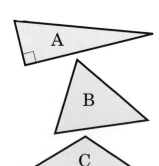

? **Can a triangle have a reflex angle?**
Can a triangle have two right angles?

Exercise

1 Look at these triangle labels.

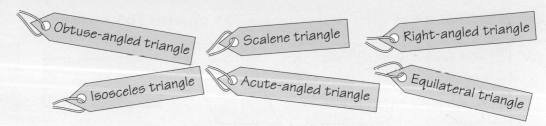

Look at these triangles.

Match two labels to each triangle.

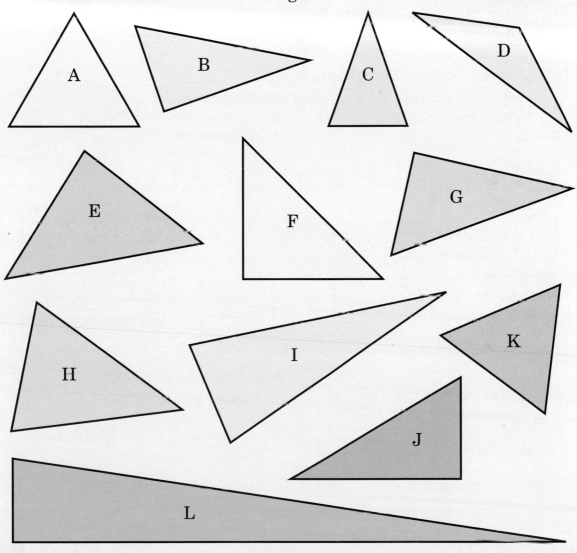

2 On squared paper draw right-angled triangles which are
(a) scalene　　　　**(b)** isosceles.

Types of quadrilateral

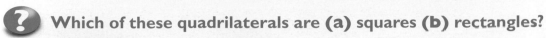

? **Which of these quadrilaterals are (a) squares (b) rectangles?**

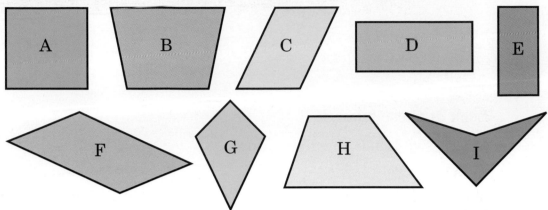

? Shape F is a parallelogram.
Opposite sides of a parallelogram are parallel.
What does 'parallel' mean?

Parallel sides

Task

Draw each of these quadrilaterals on a poster.
Label each one.

Make them much bigger for your poster.

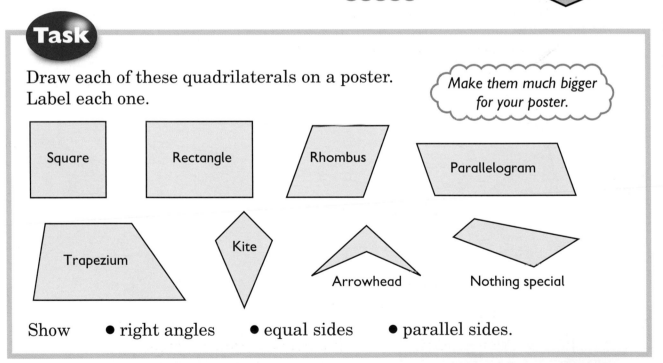

Square   Rectangle   Rhombus   Parallelogram

Trapezium   Kite   Arrowhead   Nothing special

Show   • right angles   • equal sides   • parallel sides.

? **Pete draws a quadrilateral with four right angles.**
What type of quadrilateral can it be?

Meena, draw a quadrilateral with opposite sides parallel.

? **What kinds of quadrilateral can Meena draw?**

Mrs Green

Exercise

SU

1. Copy and complete this table.

	Name of shape	How many pairs of parallel sides?	How many pairs of equal sides?
	Square	2 pairs	
		None	

SU

2. The diagram shows two sides of a quadrilateral.

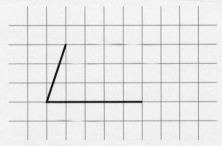

   Make four copies of the diagram on squared paper.
   Use them for parts **(a)** to **(d)**.

   (a) Add two sides to make a parallelogram.
   (b) Add two sides to make a symmetrical trapezium.
   (c) Add two sides to make a trapezium with a right angle.
   (d) Add two sides to make a different trapezium which is not symmetrical.

Tessellations

Look at this honeycomb.
It is made of cells fitted together.
The cells are **hexagons**.

? How many sides does a hexagon have?

? What can you say about
  (a) the shape of the cells
  (b) the size of the cells?

? There are no gaps between any of the cells.
How far can the pattern of cells continue?

One shape repeated to cover a surface is called a **tessellation**.
Here is one way to tessellate a triangle.

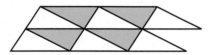

? Find another way to tessellate this triangle.

Task

I Copy this rectangle onto squared paper.
Make a tessellation using this shape.
Colour the rectangles to show the pattern.

2 (a) Copy this parallelogram onto squared paper.
Make a tessellation using this shape.
Colour the parallelogram to show the pattern.
(b) Copy the parallelogram again.
Make another **different** tessellation using
this shape.

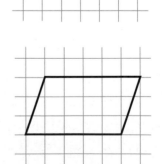

? Where do you often see patterns of tessellating rectangles?

? Can you tessellate a trapezium?

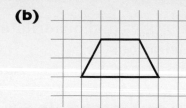

Exercise

I Copy each of these shapes onto squared paper.
Use each one for a tessellation.

(a)

(b)

Activity

This pattern was created by
M C Escher.

Escher was a Dutch artist who
lived from 1898 to 1972.

He tessellated shapes to
create pictures.

Symmetry Drawing E112 by M. C. Escher

Look at these two shapes.
The rectangle is transformed into a more
interesting shape.

(a)   **(b)**

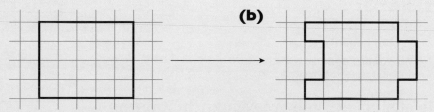

I Describe how the rectangle is changed.
Make a tessellation using the shape in **(b)**.

2 On squared paper design your own shape to tessellate.
Trace your shape onto card to make a template.
Use your template to 'tile' a piece of paper.
Decorate your tiles.

Finishing off

Now that you have finished this chapter you should be able to:

● classify triangles and quadrilaterals
● make tessellations.

Review exercise

1 Look at this pattern.
   It is made of triangles and quadrilaterals.

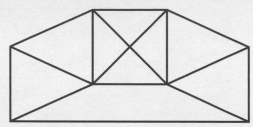

Complete this table. Only count each shape once.

Shape	How many in pattern?
Right-angled triangle	
Other isosceles triangle	
Square	1
Other parallelogram	
Other trapezium	
Kite	

Don't count the square again.

 2 The cells of a honeycomb are regular **hexagons**.
   Draw a honeycomb structure on **isometric paper**.

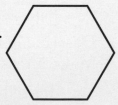

 3 **(a)** Draw x and y axes from 0 to 8.
      Plot the following points: $(2, 0)$, $(5, 0)$, $(6, 5)$ and $(3, 5)$.
      Join them to make a quadrilateral.
      Write down the name of the quadrilateral.
   (b) Repeat part **(a)** with these points $(1, 5)$, $(1, 3)$, $(4, 1)$ and $(7, 1)$.

SU

4 Copy each of these shapes onto squared paper.
Use each one for a tessellation.

(a)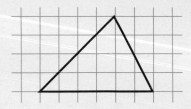

(b)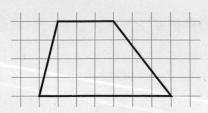

SU

5 Copy and complete this table.

	Name of shape	How many lines of symmetry?
▭	Rectangle	2
◇		
▱		
▱		
⬠		
⬠		
⌃		

13 Special numbers

Factors and primes

Sophie has 20 pansies.
There are 3 ways she can plant them.

(i)

(iii)

(ii)

1×20, 2×10 and 4×5 are the factor pairs of 20.

Sophie has 7 marigolds.

*7 is a **prime** number because it only has 2 factors: 1 and itself.*

Sophie

 How many ways are there to plant 7 marigolds?

Task

1 (a) Show how you can plant 10 of your own flowers.

(b) Write down the factor pairs of 10.

(c) Is 10 a prime number?

2 (a) Show how you can plant 11 of your flowers.

(b) Write down the factor pairs of 11.

(c) Is 11 a prime number?

3 Choose other numbers of flowers, between 12 and 20.
Do the same as in questions 1 and 2.

Sophie also grows apples.
She has 30 apples to sell.
She packs the apples into boxes.
She puts an equal number in each.

 In how many ways can she do this?

Exercise

1 **(a)** List all the prime numbers from 1 to 20.
(b) There are 2 prime numbers between 20 and 30.
What are they?

> *1 is not a **prime** number because it only has one factor.*

2 **(a)** Copy and complete these.

$1 \times = 24$ $\qquad$ $2 \times = 24$

$3 \times = 24$ $\qquad$ $4 \times = 24$

(b) List the factors of 24.
(c) Explain why 24 is not a prime number.

3 What factor pair is missing for the number 40?

1×40 $\qquad$ 2×20 $\qquad$ 4×10

4 **(a)** Which factor pair is wrong for the number 36?

1×36 $\qquad$ 2×18 $\qquad$ 3×12 $\qquad$ 4×8 $\qquad$ 6×6

(b) What should it be?

5 **(a)** Copy and complete this calculation in as many ways as you can.

$ \times = 50$

(b) Is 50 a prime number?

6 Which of these numbers are prime?

5 $\qquad$ 19 $\qquad$ 27 $\qquad$ 37 $\qquad$ 39 $\qquad$ 46

Activity Work through the numbers from 30 to 100.
Sort the numbers into the two groups below.
You can use a calculator to help you.

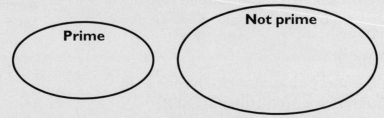

Prime

Not prime

Multiples

Christina makes some triangles with matchsticks.

Length of side	1	2	3	4	5
Number of matchsticks	3	6	9	12	15

It is the 3 times table.

*Yes they are **multiples** of 3.*

Christina

Mrs Green

? **How many matchsticks are there in the 6th triangle?**
What about the 10th triangle?

Task

Christina now makes squares with matchsticks.

1 Draw the first 5 squares.
  Write the number of matchsticks below each diagram.

2 Copy and complete this table.

Length of side	1	2	3	4	5
Number of matchsticks	4				

3 What kind of numbers are these answers?

4 How many matchsticks are there in the next square?

5 How many matchsticks are there in the 100th square?

Show how you get your answers.

6 Christina makes some other shapes.
  Investigate the number of matchsticks for:
  (a) hexagons **(b)** pentagons.

A pentagon has 5 sides.

Christina makes some more matchstick shapes.
The numbers of matchsticks are multiples of 8.

 What does her shape look like?

Exercise

1 Christina makes L-shapes with matchsticks.

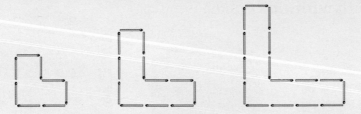

(a) Draw the next 2 diagrams.

(b) Copy and complete this table.

Height of L-shape	2	3	4	5	6
Number of matchsticks					

(c) Copy and complete this sentence.

These numbers are ▮▮▮▮▮▮ of 4.

(d) The number of matchsticks increase by 4 each time. Why is this?

(e) Christina makes an L-shape of height 10. How many matchsticks does she use?

(f) Christina has 100 matchsticks. She makes the biggest L-shape possible. What is the height of the L-shape?

2 Christina now makes cross shapes with matchsticks.

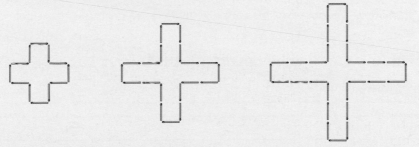

(a) Copy these diagrams and draw the next 2.

(b) Write the number of matchsticks underneath each diagram.

(c) What do you notice?

Activity Ice-creams cost 99p.
Work out how much it costs for 2 ice-creams, then 3, then 4, etc.
Work up as far as 10, or more.

Squares and cubes

Jo makes some cubes with multilink cubes.

   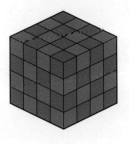 

Jo looks at one face on each cube.
She works out the number of small squares.
She puts her answers in a table.

Length of Side	Number of squares on 1 face
1	$1 \times 1 = 1^2 = 1$
2	$2 \times 2 = 2^2 = 4$
3	$3 \times 3 = 3^2 = 9$

? **What are the next 2 rows in Jo's table?**

? **Look at the answers.**
What type of numbers are these?

Task

Work out how many small cubes make up the bigger cubes.

1 Copy and complete this table.

Length of Side	1	2	3	4	5	6
Workings	$1^3 = 1 \times 1 \times 1$	$2^3 = 2 \times 2 \times 2$	$3^3 =$			
Total number of small cubes	1					

2 A cube has sides of length 10.
How many small cubes are in it?

3 You have 512 small cubes.
What is the biggest cube you can make with them?

These are called **cube numbers**.

? **What is 1000^2? What is 100^3?**

Exercise

1. (a) Work out these.
   (i) 6×6
   (ii) 9×9
   (iii) 2^2
   (iv) 4^2
   (b) What sort of numbers are your answers?

2. (a) Work out these.
   (i) $5 \times 5 \times 5$
   (ii) $2 \times 2 \times 2$
   (iii) 3^3
   (iv) 1^3
   (b) What sort of numbers are your answers?

3. Which of these numbers are square numbers?

   | 6 | 9 | 22 | 25 | 45 | 64 | 100 |

4. Which of these is a cube number?

   | 10 | 100 | 1000 |

5. Jo is wrong. How can you tell?

   82 is a square number.

6. (a) What number is squared to get 49?
   (b) What number is cubed to get 27?

7. Which numbers between 1 and 100 are both a square and a cube number?

8. Copy and complete these.
   (a) $9 = \boxed{}^2$
   (b) $25 = \boxed{}^2$
   (c) $100 = \boxed{}^2$

9. Copy and complete these.
   (a) $8 = \boxed{}^3$
   (b) $216 = \boxed{}^3$
   (c) $1000 = \boxed{}^3$

Investigation

You have 100 multilink cubes.
Make as many different cubes as you can.
Try to use all the cubes.

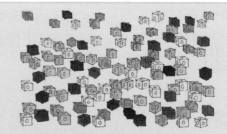

Powers of 2

Look at this chain.

Humza shows how to get the numbers in the chain.

Humza

This is taking me a long time.

$$2 = 2$$
$$2 \times 2 = 4$$
$$2 \times 2 \times 2 = 8$$
$$2 \times 2 \times 2 \times 2 = 16$$
$$2 \times 2 \times 2 \times 2 \times 2 = 32$$

*A quick way to write $2 \times 2 \times 2 \times 2 \times 2$ is 2^5. You say **2 to the power 5**.*

Mrs Green

? **Write out Humza's sums again using powers of 2.**

Task

Michelle wins a prize in a competition.
She must choose her prize.

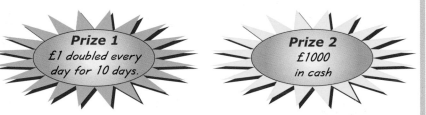

Prize 1
£1 doubled every day for 10 days.

Prize 2
£1000 in cash

I (a) She makes a table to work out prize 1. Copy and complete the table.

(b) Which is the better prize?

Number of days	Prize in £	Power of 2
1	1	2^0
2	2	2^1
3	3	2^2
4		
5		
6		
7		
8		
9		
10		

2 Another competition doubles £1 for 20 days.
Work out the value of this prize.

? **Look at the patterns in your numbers.**
What is the value of 2^0? What about 2^{-1}?

Exercise

1. Write these as powers of 2.
   (a) $2 \times 2 \times 2 \times 2$ (b) $2 \times 2 \times 2 \times 2 \times 2 \times 2 \times 2$
   (c) $2 \times 2 \times 2 \times 2 \times 2 \times 2 \times 2 \times 2 \times 2 \times 2 \times 2 \times 2$

2. Work out the value of the numbers in question 1.

   > Use your table from the task to help you.

3. Write these numbers as multiplications.
   (a) 2^2 (b) 2^6 (c) 2^{10}

4. Work out the value of the numbers in question 3.

5. Use Meena's calculation to work out
   (a) 2^{19} (b) 2^{17}

> $2^{18} = 262\,144$

Meena

6. Jack's calculation is wrong.
   Look at his answer.
   How can you tell it is wrong?

> $2^{24} = 33\,544\,433$

Jack

Activity

How many names do you know for powers of 10?
Some letters have been filled in to help you.

> Did you know 10^{100} is called a googol?

$10^2 = 10 \times 10 = 100$ | H | | | D | | | D |

$10^3 = 10 \times 10 \times 10 = 1000$ | | H | | U | | | | D |

$10^6 = 10 \times 10 \times 10 \times 10 \times 10 \times 10 = 1\,000\,000$

| | I | | | I | | N |

$10^9 = 10 \times 10 \times 10 \times 10 \times 10 \times 10 \times 10 \times 10 \times 10 = 1\,000\,000\,000$

| | | L | L | | | |

$10^{12} = 10 \times 10 \times 10 \times 10 \times 10 \times 10 \times 10 \times 10 \times 10 \times 10 \times 10 \times 10$
$= 1\,000\,000\,000\,000$

| T | | | L | | | O | |

Finishing off

Now that you have finished this chapter you should know:

- the meaning of the terms factor, factor pair, prime number, multiple, square number, cube number, power of 2.

Review exercise

1 Write down
- **(a)** 5 multiples of 6
- **(b)** 5 factors of 100
- **(c)** 5 square numbers
- **(d)** 5 cube numbers
- **(e)** 5 powers of 2.

Give me 5.

Kim's Dad

2 Which of these statements are true for the number 16?

It is a multiple of 4.	One of its factors is 8.	It is a prime number.
It is a square number.	It is a cube number.	It is a power of 2.

SU

3 **(a)** For each number along the bottom, shade or colour the boxes to show the factors.
The first 3 numbers have been done for you.

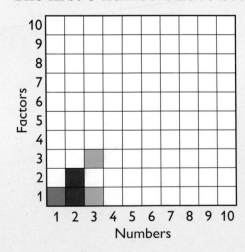

(b) What patterns do you notice?

4 **(a)** Copy and complete this table.
Use your diagram from question 3 to help you.

Number	Number of factors
1	1
2	2
3	2
4	
5	
6	
7	
8	
9	
10	

(b) List the numbers which have only 2 factors.
(c) What type of numbers are these?
(d) List the numbers with an odd number of factors.
(e) What type of numbers are these?

5 Are these statements true or false?
(a) All prime numbers are odd.
(b) All square numbers are even.
(c) All cube numbers are odd.
(d) All multiples of 2 are even.
(e) All multiples of 3 are odd.
(f) 2^{27} is even.

Investigation

SU This is Pascal's triangle.

1 On a copy of the diagram colour
all the multiples of 2.
What patterns do you notice?

2 On another copy of the diagram
colour all the multiples of 5.
What patterns do you notice?

3 Choose another number
between 1 and 10. Do the
same.

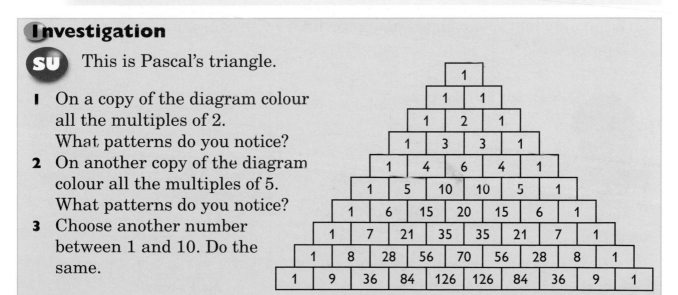

SU Class 8G have another Reward lesson.

You can play **Alien attack**.

Mr Smith

Alien attack

Jack and Mark play Alien attack.
They cannot see each other's boards.

Look at the **Alien attack** board.
Jack is defending the target.

I have put out my space mines to catch Mark. If a space ship crosses over one, it is blown up!

Jack

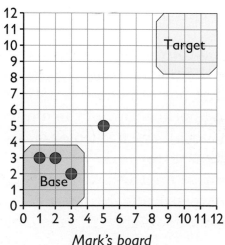

Jack's board

Mark can only move four places along the lines in any turn.

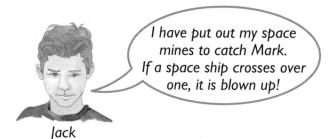

I am starting at (3, 3). I am moving one counter east to (5, 3) and then north to (5, 5).

At the start Mark's pieces can be anywhere in the Base.

Mark

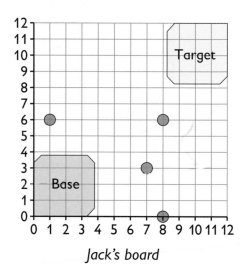

Mark's board

? **Is this a safe move for Mark?**

After each of Mark's moves, Jack can move one space mine two
places along the lines.

Mark is at (5, 5) so I need to move one of my mines. Think! Where will he go next?

Juck

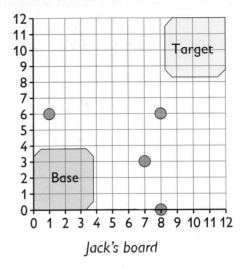

Jack's board

? **Which counter should Jack move?**

I'm starting another counter from (1, 3) and moving north to (1, 7).

Mark

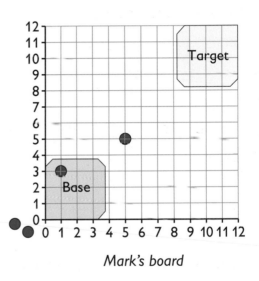

Mark's board

? **What happens next?**

To win, Jack must blow up all Mark's space ships.
If Mark reaches the target with one counter, he wins.

Task

Play **Alien attack** with a friend.
Play 3 games attacking and 3 games defending.
Keep the score of who wins most games.

Looking at questionnaires

Answer the questions on this questionnaire.

1 How did you travel to school today?

☐   ☐   ☐   ☐   ☐

Car   *Bus*   *Bike*   *Walk*   *Other*

2 How many children are there in your family?

☐   ☐   ☐   ☐   ☐

1   *2*   *3*   *4*   *More than 4*

3 Do you have school lunches?

☐   ☐   ☐   ☐

Every day   *Most days*   *Sometimes*   *Never*

4 Are you left-handed?

☐   ☐

Yes   *No*

? **Did you find any of the questions difficult to answer?**

Task

1 Collect the results of the survey from your class.

> *Choose from the diagrams you used in Chapter 4.*

2 Draw a diagram to display the results for each question.
3 Make a poster to show the results of the survey.
4 Think of 2 more questions to ask the class.
5 Add the results of these to your poster.

Look back at the questionnaire.

? **Why is the *Other* response needed in question 1?**

? **Are there enough responses in question 3?**

Exercise

1 Karl has written a list of questions and a list of responses.
Match the questions with the responses.

> **Questions**
>
> **(a)** How many magazines do you buy each week?
>
> **(b)** Do you wear a helmet when you cycle?
>
> **(c)** Are you over 18?
>
> **(d)** What do you think of your school lunches?

> **Responses**
>
> **(i)** Always ☐   Sometimes ☐   Never ☐
>
> **(ii)** Yes ☐   No ☐
>
> **(iii)** Very good ☐   Good ☐
>
>   Average ☐   Poor ☐
>
>   Very poor ☐
>
> **(iv)** None ☐   1 ☐   2–4 ☐
>
>   More than 4 ☐

2 **(a)** What is wrong with this question?

> How old are you?
>
> 0–10 ☐   10–20 ☐
>
> 20–25 ☐   50–80 ☐

I am 95.

I am 10.

(b) Write a better question.

3 This question needs another response.
What should it say?

It's OK but nothing special.

> What do you think of this new flavour of ice-cream?
>
> Very good ☐   Good ☐   Poor ☐   Very poor ☐

4 This question does not have enough responses.
What other responses should there be?

> How many days did you play football last week?
>
> 1 ☐   2 ☐   4 ☐   More than 5 ☐

Good survey questions

You are going to carry out a survey of your own.
Write a questionnaire to find out what students think about school lunches.
The first 3 questions are written for you.

I What do you usually do for lunch?

Eat lunch at school ☐   Eat sandwiches ☐   Go home ☐

? **You need to add another response.**
What should it say?

I buy chips from the fish and chip shop.

Ali

2 Do you think there is enough choice?

Yes, plenty ☐   About right ☐   No, not enough ☐

Make sure all opinions are given.

3 How much do you spend on your lunch?

Less than £1 ☐   £1–£2 ☐   More than £2 ☐

I spend £1. Which box do I tick?

John

Task

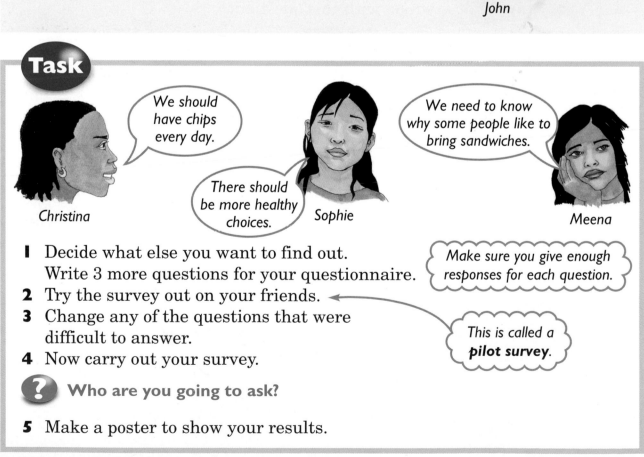

We should have chips every day.

Christina

There should be more healthy choices.

Sophie

We need to know why some people like to bring sandwiches.

Meena

I Decide what else you want to find out.
Write 3 more questions for your questionnaire.

Make sure you give enough responses for each question.

2 Try the survey out on your friends.

3 Change any of the questions that were difficult to answer.

This is called a pilot survey.

4 Now carry out your survey.

? **Who are you going to ask?**

5 Make a poster to show your results.

Exercise

1 Michelle has written these questions for a questionnaire.
She hasn't written any responses.
Write the responses for Michelle.

Michelle

> **(a)** Do you own a bike?
>
> **(b)** Do you like chocolate?
>
> **(c)** How many chocolate bars do you eat in a week?
>
> **(d)** What do you think of your school uniform?
>
> **(e)** How many miles do you travel to school?
>
> **(f)** Do you think fox hunting should be banned?

2 Write a question for each of these situations.
Write responses for each question.

(a) Your teacher wants to know how long students spent doing their homework last night.

(b) You want to know how much pocket money the students in your class are given.

(c) A supermarket wants to know if people think their own brand of coffee is as good as the leading brand.

(d) You want to know the favourite type of music of the students in your class.

Finishing off

Now that you have finished this chapter you should be able to:

● write good questions for a survey.

Review exercise

You are going to do a survey about the activities available at your school.

1

I don't do any activities.

Alan

I go to something every lunchtime.

Mark

Write a question to find out how many activities students go to each week.

2
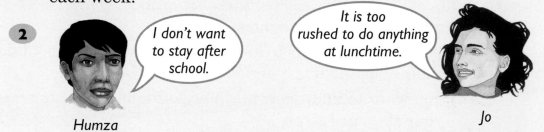

I don't want to stay after school.

Humza

It is too rushed to do anything at lunchtime.

Jo

Write a question to find out the best time to hold an activity.

3

There is nothing to do if you are not sporty.

Michelle

I sing in the choir and play in the orchestra.

Lucy

Write a question to find out the type of activities that people go to.

4

We should have a homework club.

Pete

Find out people's opinions of a homework club.

5

Harry: *I want a computer club.*

Mercy: *I want to listen to music at lunchtime.*

Tim: *There is nothing I enjoy doing.*

Kim: *I am happy to read in the library.*

Jack: *The older children are always using the computers.*

Think of some information that is useful for your survey.
Write questions to find this information.

6 Try out your questions on your friends.

Megan: *There isn't a box for my answer.*

Karl: *I don't understand this question.*

Do you need to change any questions?

7 Carry out your survey.

8 Collect your results.

Meena: *We need to use frequency tables.*

9 Draw diagrams to show the answers to your questions.

Ali: *Should we use a pie chart or a bar chart?*

10 Display your results on a poster.

Ratios

Sophie and Tim buy posters.

Sophie

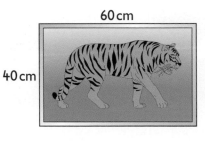
60 cm

40 cm   30 cm

20 cm

Tim

 How much bigger is Tim's poster than Sophie's?

Task

1 Make copies of these patterns on dotted paper. Make them twice as big.

(a) 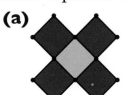   **(b)** 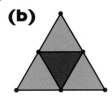   **(c)**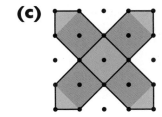

(d) 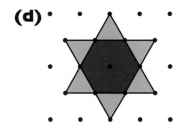   **(e)**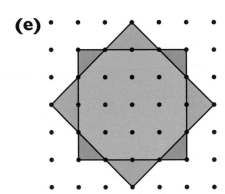

2 Colour your patterns to match these.

The shapes are in the same ratio.
The ratio is 1 : 2.
The copy is twice the size of the original.
The ratios 30 : 60 and 20 : 40 are the same as the ratio 1 : 2.

 How do you know?   **?** **When are two ratios the same?**

Exercise

1 These shapes are in the ratio 1 : 3.
The copy is three times the size
of the original.
Write down the ratio of sizes of
each of these.

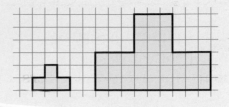

(a) 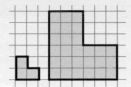   **(b)** 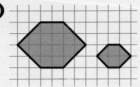   **(c)**

(d)    **(e)** 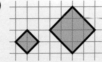   **(f)**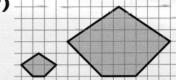

2 In each part one ratio is different from the other two.
Find the odd one out.

(a) 2 : 4   4 : 6   5 : 10   **(b)** 1 : 2   7 : 14   5 : 12

(c) 1 : 3   3 : 9   2 : 4   **(d)** 1 : 7   2 : 12   3 : 18

(e) 2 : 10   5 : 50   4 : 20   **(f)** 5 : 30   4 : 20   7 : 35

Activity

This is a rough plan of Humza's bedroom.

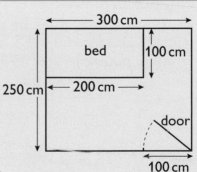

Draw the plan accurately.
Use the scale of 1 : 10.

*Divide each
measurement by 10.*

What other furniture might Humza have?
Decide on its measurements.
Add it to your plan.

Using ratio

John is planning a party
for 12 people.
This recipe is for 4 people.

Pizza base (4 people)

250 g flour
$\frac{1}{2}$ teaspoon yeast
$\frac{1}{2}$ teaspoon salt
175 ml water
1 tablespoon olive oil

*I need enough
for 12 people.*

John

? **What quantities does John need?**

? **What is the ratio of the quantities, *amount in recipe : amount used*?**

Task

1 This recipe is for 6 muffins.
Copy and complete the table so that John has 12 muffins.

Recipe	Working for ratio 1:2	Amount needed
1 egg		
62 g yoghurt	62 × 2	124 g yoghurt
62 ml milk		
125 g flour		
125 g sugar		
37 g cocoa		

2 John needs to have every recipe for 12 people.
What quantities does he need for these recipes? Make up tables.

Dhal (2 people)

2 tablespoons olive oil
1 onion
1 teaspoon curry powder
125 g red lentils
450 ml stock

Egg fried rice (3 people)

80 g rice
1 tablespoon olive oil
20 g bacon
1 egg
45 g beansprouts

John finds a recipe for flapjacks.
It is for 24 flapjacks.

Flapjacks (24 flapjacks)

120 g butter
90 g golden syrup
90 g brown sugar
250 g rolled oats

 **What quantities does John need
for 12 flapjacks?**

Exercise

1 Ali visits relatives in Canada.
Her money is in Canadian dollars.
2 dollars = £1
Find the cost in pounds of
(a) a book for 12 dollars
(b) a camera for 80 dollars
(c) a meal for 30 dollars.

2 dollars = £1

Ali

2 Sophie goes to Spain for her holiday.
Her money is in euros.
3 euros = £2
Find the cost in pounds of
(a) a meal for 30 euros
(b) a pair of jeans for 24 euros
(c) a CD for 15 euros.

3 euros = £2

Sophie

3 A litre of paint covers 12 m².
(a) Wayne has to cover 36 m² in his bedroom.
How many litres does he need?
(b) Samir has to cover 24 m² in his bedroom.
How many litres does he need?

4 Michelle finds these deals.

I spend 30 minutes on the Internet each day.

Michelle

Deal A
1 p per minute

Deal B
70 p per hour

Deal C
£7 per month

What is the cost of each deal for 1 day?

A month is 4 weeks.

Sharing in a given ratio

There are 4 members of the Jones family and 2 of the Smith family.
They go out for a meal together.
They share the bill of £60.

? How much does the Jones family pay?
How much does the Smith family pay?

? What is the ratio of the amounts the families pay?
What fraction does each family pay?

Task

1 The Jones family of 4 are now on holiday with the 2 Smiths.
They share the costs.
Copy and complete this table.

Item	Cost	Fraction paid by Jones family	Amount paid by Jones family	Fraction paid by Smith family	Amount paid by Smith family
Hiring a car	£240	$\frac{2}{3}$	$\frac{2}{3} \times £240 = $	$\frac{1}{3}$	
Buying petrol	£90				
Buying food	£150				
Hiring surfboards	£75				

2 Some other families go on holiday together.
Make new tables to show how much each family pays.
The items and costs are the same as in the table above.
(a) There are 3 members of the Singh family and 2 of the Brown family.
(b) There are 4 members of the O'Leary family and just 1 of the Scott family.

? Which of these numbers can be shared exactly in the ratio 3 : 4?
Explain why.

14   240   90   140   75

Exercise

1 Share these in the ratio 1 : 2.
  (a) 15   **(b)** 9   **(c)** 24

2 Share these in the ratio 3 : 1.
  (a) 12   **(b)** 40   **(c)** 28

3 36 students filled in this questionnaire.
These pie charts show the answers.

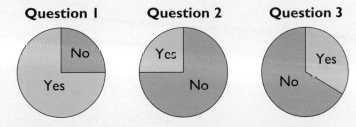

How many said yes for each question?
How many said no?

1 Do you have a mobile phone?
  Yes ☐   No ☐

2 Do you have a computer?
  Yes ☐   No ☐

3 Do you have your own TV?
  Yes ☐   No ☐

4

Do you support Arsenal?

Alan

Do you support Manchester United?

Tim

In a school twice as many students support Manchester United as
any other team. The ratio is 2 : 1.
  (a) Divide 360° in the ratio 2 : 1.
  (b) Draw a pie chart.

Activity   **1** Ask your friends some questions.
        2 Draw pie charts to show the answers.

Finishing off

Now that you have finished this chapter you should be able to:

- use ratio notation
- apply ratio to problems
- share in a given ratio.

Review exercise

1 Draw copies of this shape to scale. Use these ratios.
(a) $1:2$ **(b)** $1:3$ **(c)** $2:1$

2 What quantities are needed for 8 people?

Chocolate ice-cream (4 people)

4 egg yolks
300 ml milk
300 ml double cream
130 g chocolate

3 Lucy visits relatives in Barbados.
Her money is in Barbados dollars.

3 dollars = £1

Lucy

Find the cost in pounds of
(a) a T-shirt for 12 dollars
(b) a meal for 30 dollars
(c) a hat for 21 dollars.

4 Share 30 in the ratio
(a) $1:2$ **(b)** $1:4$
(c) $2:1$ **(d)** $2:3$

5 Copy the boxes **(a)**, **(b)** and **(c)** and write each of these ratios in one of the boxes.
All the ratios in each box must be the same.

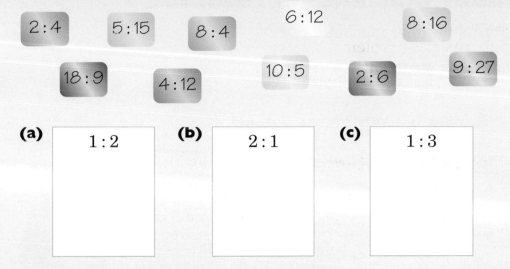

$2:4$ $5:15$ $8:4$ $6:12$ $8:16$
$18:9$ $4:12$ $10:5$ $2:6$ $9:27$

(a)

$1:2$

(b)

$2:1$

(c)

$1:3$

Make up some more ratios for each box.

6 Mercy is on a cycling holiday in France.
The distances on these signs are in kilometres.
Write the distances in miles.

8 kilometres = 5 miles

Mercy

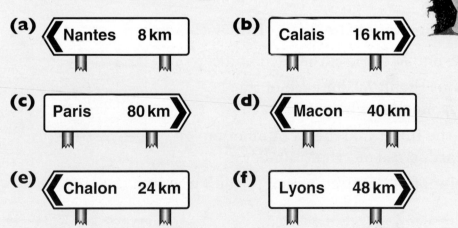

(a) Nantes   8 km

(b) Calais   16 km

(c) Paris   80 km

(d) Macon   40 km

(e) Chalon   24 km

(f) Lyons   48 km

Activity   You need a map of France.

1 Plan a journey of about 1000 kilometres.

2 Write down all the distances in kilometres.

3 Change the distances to miles.

Number machines in reverse

Look at this number machine.

Input ⟶ + 5 ⟶ Output

? The input is 3. What is the output?

? The output is 12. How can you work out the input?

Kim **reverses** the number machine.

⬜ ⟵ − 5 ⟵ 12

To **undo** add 5, you subtract 5.

Kim

? What is the missing number?

? How do you undo these?

(a) subtract 6   **(b)** add 4   **(c)** multiply by 3   **(d)** divide by 2

Task

Play **Number machine 3-in-a-line** with a friend.

- Choose one of these cards each and copy it.
- Work out the input for each of the number machines below.
- When the input matches a number on your card, cross out that number.
- The winner is the first person to get 3 in a line.

4	1	21
3	11	8
10	14	16

8	7	10
6	4	3
2	11	21

1 ⬜ ⟶ + 3 ⟶ 7

2 ⬜ ⟶ − 2 ⟶ 8

3 ⬜ ⟶ × 3 ⟶ 33

4 ⬜ ⟶ ÷ 4 ⟶ 2

5 ⬜ ⟶ − 15 ⟶ 1

6 ⬜ ⟶ × 5 ⟶ 10

? What is the input for this number machine?

⬜ ⟶ × 3 ⟶ + 1 ⟶ 13

Exercise

SU

1 **(a)** Draw the **reverse** of each of these number machines.

(i) [ ] ⟶ [+ 4] ⟶ [4]

(ii) [ ] ⟶ [− 7] ⟶ [29]

(iii) [ ] ⟶ [+ 16] ⟶ [24]

(iv) [ ] ⟶ [− 17] ⟶ [32]

(b) Now find the missing numbers.

SU

2 **(a)** Draw the **reverse** of each of these number machines.

(i) [ ] ⟶ [× 3] ⟶ [15]

(ii) [ ] ⟶ [× 8] ⟶ [48]

(iii) [ ] ⟶ [÷ 3] ⟶ [2]

(iv) [ ] ⟶ [÷ 9] ⟶ [4]

(b) Now find the missing numbers.

3 Look at this number machine.

[Input] ⟶ [+ 3] ⟶ [Output]

Find the missing numbers in this table.

Input	1	2			
Output			6	7	10

4 Michelle has a Saturday job.
This number machine shows how her pay is worked out.

[Number of hours worked] ⟶ [× 3] ⟶ [Pay in pounds]

How many hours has she worked when she is paid
(a) £6   **(b)** £9   **(c)** £33   **(d)** £4.50?

Using letters

John and Christina are playing the **Think of a number** game.

John: I think of a number. Multiply it by 3. The answer is 21.

John

Christina: Let me write this down.

Christina

Christina writes: $3 \times n = 21$

This is an **equation**. There is only one number that n could be.

? **What does n stand for?**
Are $3 \times n$, $n \times 3$ and $3n$ all the same?
How do you undo '$\times 3$'?

Christina writes: $n = 21 \div 3$
So $n = 7$

Christina has **solved** the equation.

? **How would you solve these equations?**
(a) $n + 3 = 21$ **(b)** $n - 3 = 21$ **(c)** $n \div 3 = 21$

Task

1 Solve these equations.
(a) $n + 3 = 6$ **(b)** $n + 7 = 12$ **(c)** $4 + n = 15$
(d) $n - 5 = 8$ **(e)** $n - 2 = 13$ **(f)** $n - 20 = 1$
(g) $3n = 12$ **(h)** $2n = 14$ **(i)** $5n = 30$
(j) $n \div 3 = 2$ **(k)** $n \div 2 = 3$ **(l)** $n \div 4 = 1$

2 Play **Think of a number** with a friend.
● Think of a number and give your friend a clue like John did.
● Write an equation for your friend's clue like Christina did.
● Solve your equation.
Show your working like Christina did.

? **How can you check you have the right answer?**

Exercise

1 Solve these equations.

    (a) $a + 5 = 7$ **(b)** $b + 3 = 4$

    (c) $7 + c = 11$ **(d)** $3 + d = 4$

    (e) $7 + e = 9$ **(f)** $f + 9 = 20$

2 Solve these equations.

    (a) $a - 3 = 6$ **(b)** $b - 5 = 5$

    (c) $c - 8 = 1$ **(d)** $d - 4 = 10$

    (e) $e - 1 = 1$ **(f)** $f - 5 = 0$

3 Solve these equations.

    (a) $2 \times a = 8$ **(b)** $3 \times b = 15$

    (c) $4 \times c = 20$ **(d)** $2d = 10$

    (e) $5e = 25$ **(f)** $7f = 21$

4 Solve these equations.

    (a) $n \div 3 = 6$ **(b)** $n \div 7 = 3$ **(c)** $n \div 2 = 15$

5 Solve these equations.

    (a) $n + 4 = 9$ **(b)** $n - 3 = 2$ **(c)** $1 + n = 3$

    (d) $n \div 5 = 8$ **(e)** $7n = 14$ **(f)** $10n = 10$

    (g) $n \div 3 = 12$ **(h)** $2 + n = 17$ **(i)** $n - 7 = 15$

6 Alan and Jo are playing **Think of a number**.

I think of a number. Multiply it by 7. The answer is 35.

Alan

I think of a number. Subtract 12. The answer is 8.

Jo

    (a) Write down an equation for Alan's number.

    (b) Solve your equation.

    (c) Write down an equation for Jo's number.

    (d) Solve your equation.

    (e) How can you check your answers?

Balancing equations

Look at these scales.

The left side balances the right side.

Samir wants to find out the weight of
each package.

> They are
> the same.

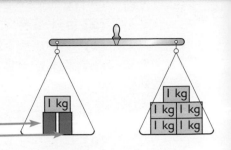

Samir writes:

> Weight of 2 packages + 1 kg = 5 kg
> So   2W + 1 = 5

Look at Samir's working.

> 2W + 1 = 5
> Take 1 from both sides: 2W = 4

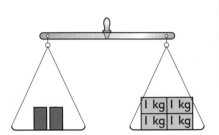

? **Explain Samir's working.**
What has he done to the scales?
Now solve the equation.

Task

Make a poster. Call it 'Solving an equation by balancing'.
Solve each of the 2 problems below on your poster.

● Write an equation for the scales.

● Solve your equation.

● Draw the scales at each stage of your working,
as Samir did.

> Make sure you show
> all your working.

● Check your answer.

1 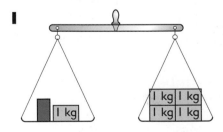   **2**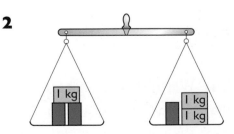

? **You always do the same thing to both sides of an equation. Why?**

Exercise

For each set of scales
- write an equation
- solve your equation
- show all your working
- draw the scales at each stage of your working, as Samir did
- check your answer is right.

1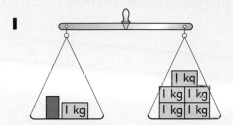

2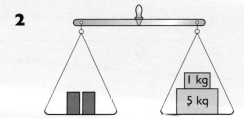

3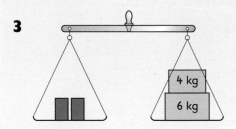

4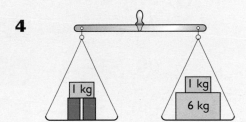

5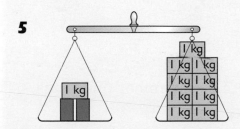

6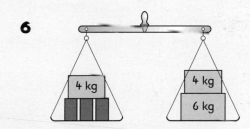

7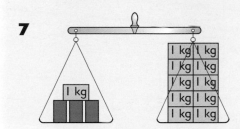

8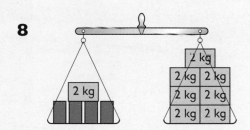

9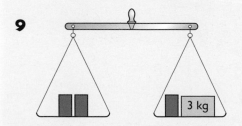

10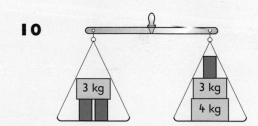

Finishing off

Now that you have finished this chapter you should:

- know what a number machine is
- be able to reverse a number machine to find the input
- know what an equation is
- be able to write down an equation for a **Think of a number** problem
- be able to solve an equation by balancing.

Review exercise

1 **(a)** Draw the reverse of each of these number machines.

(i) ☐ ⟶ + 7 ⟶ 12

(ii) ☐ ⟶ − 4 ⟶ 1

(iii) ☐ ⟶ + 8 ⟶ 16

(iv) ☐ ⟶ − 3 ⟶ 3

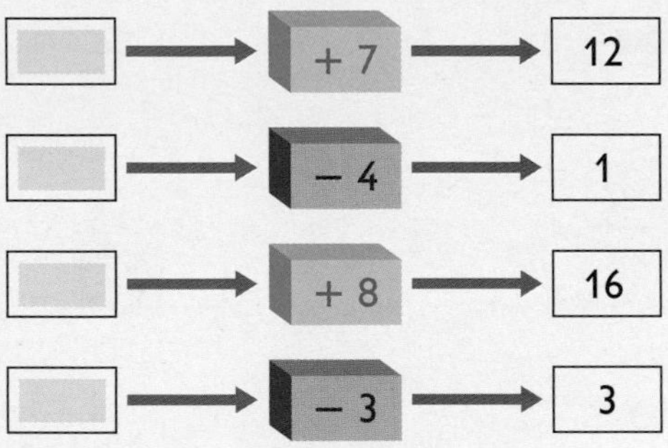

(b) Now find the missing numbers.

2 **(a)** Draw the reverse of each of these number machines.

(i) ☐ ⟶ × 2 ⟶ 20

(ii) ☐ ⟶ ÷ 2 ⟶ 2

(iii) ☐ ⟶ × 4 ⟶ 4

(iv) ☐ ⟶ ÷ 7 ⟶ 3

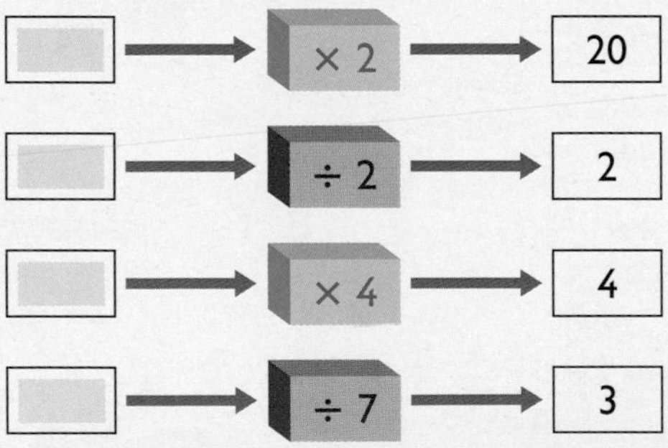

(b) Now find the missing numbers.

3 Solve these equations.

(a) $a + 9 = 12$ **(b)** $b + 5 = 7$

(c) $8 + c = 15$ **(d)** $d - 1 = 5$

(e) $e - 6 = 1$ **(f)** $f - 3 = 3$

4 Solve these equations.
   (a) $2a = 12$ **(b)** $3b = 12$ **(c)** $4c = 12$
   (d) $d \div 2 = 8$ **(e)** $e \div 5 = 9$ **(f)** $f \div 3 = 1$

5 Solve these equations.
   (a) $n + 2 = 3$ **(b)** $n - 1 = 4$ **(c)** $2 + n = 13$
   (d) $n \div 3 = 8$ **(e)** $2n = 24$ **(f)** $4n = 16$
   (g) $n \div 7 = 2$ **(h)** $5 + n = 6$ **(i)** $n - 1 = 3$

6 Pete and Ali are playing the **Think of a number** game.

I think of a number. Multiply it by 4. The answer is 28.

Pete

I think of a number. Subtract 3. The answer is 1.

Ali

   (a) Write down an equation for Pete's number.
   (b) Solve your equation.
   (c) Write down an equation for Ali's number.
   (d) Solve your equation.

SU

7 For each set of scales
   • write down an equation
   • solve your equation
   • show all your working
   • draw the scales at each stage of your working
   • check your answer is right.

   (a)

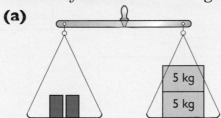

   (b)

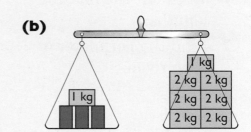

   (c)

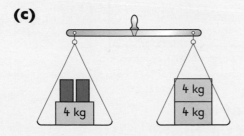

   (d)

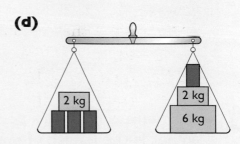

Perimeter

Kim

How many rolls of wallpaper do we need to decorate the living room, Dad?

It depends on the perimeter of the room.

Kim's Dad

? How can they find the perimeter?

Kim measures the walls.
She draws a plan.

I can work out the lengths of the other walls.

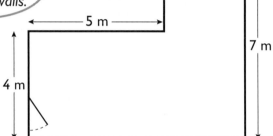

5 m · 7 m · 4 m · 8 m

? How long are the walls?

? What is the perimeter of the room?

Task

This is a sketch plan of the upstairs of Kim's house.

1 Work out the missing lengths.
2 Find the perimeter of each room.

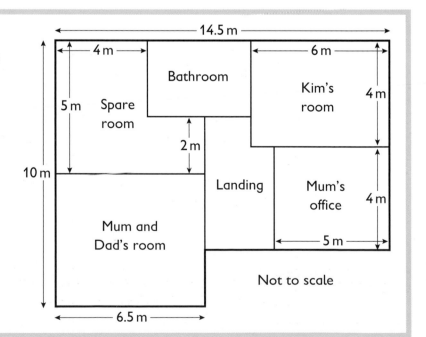

14.5 m

4 m · Bathroom · 6 m · Kim's room · 4 m

5 m · Spare room

2 m

10 m · Landing · Mum's office · 4 m

5 m

Mum and Dad's room

6.5 m

Not to scale

? A square room has a perimeter of 16 m.
What is the length of one wall of the room?

Exercise

1 Work out the perimeter of each of these shapes.

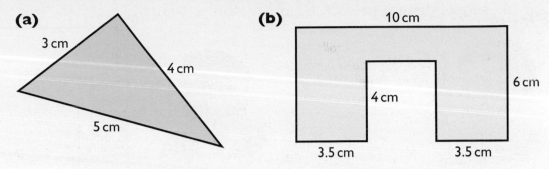

(a)

3 cm

4 cm

5 cm

(b)

10 cm

6 cm

4 cm

3.5 cm   3.5 cm

2 This is a sketch plan of a house and garden.

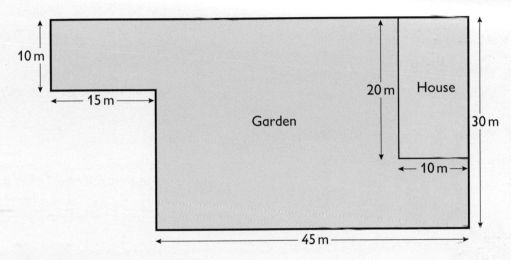

10 m

15 m

Garden

20 m

House

10 m

30 m

45 m

(a) Work out the missing lengths.
(b) Work out the perimeter of the garden.

3 **(a)** A square garden has a perimeter of 120 metres.
   How long is each side of the garden?
(b) A classroom is a rectangle, 15 m long.
   The perimeter of the room is 50 m.
   How wide is the classroom?

Activity   Use a ruler and compasses to **construct** 3 **different** triangles,
each with a perimeter of 18 cm.

Area

For his school design project, Samir makes a T-shirt.

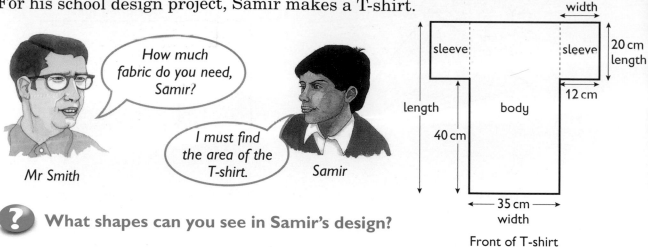

How much fabric do you need, Samir?

Mr Smith

I must find the area of the T-shirt.

Samir

Front of T-shirt

? **What shapes can you see in Samir's design?**

? **What is the area of one sleeve? What about two sleeves?**

Remember: Area of a rectangle = length × width.

? **What is the area of the body?**

? **What is the total area of Samir's T-shirt?**

Remember a T-shirt has a front and a back!

Task

1 Sketch a T-shirt with measurements to fit you.

2 Work out how much fabric you need to make it.

3 Choose a suitable scale and make a scale drawing of your T-shirt.

4 On your scale drawing, design and colour a logo for the front of the T-shirt.

5 Put all the class designs together to make a display.

? **How much green fabric would Samir need to make this tablecloth?**

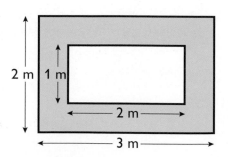

Exercise

1 Look at this shape.
  (a) Find the area of part A.
  (b) Find the area of part B.
  (c) What is the area of the whole shape?

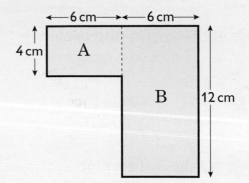

2 Find the areas of these shapes.

(a)

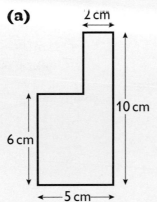

(b)

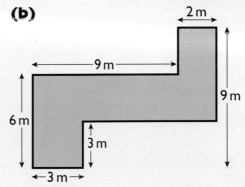

3 This is Karl's garden.
  (a) Find the area of the whole garden.
  (b) Find the area of the patio.
  (c) What is the area of the grass?

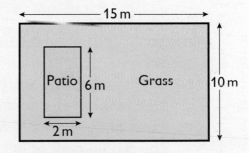

4 This letter E is painted on the side of a van.

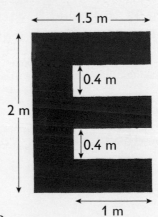

What is the area of the painted letter?

Volume

This is the swimming pool at
Avonford Leisure Centre.

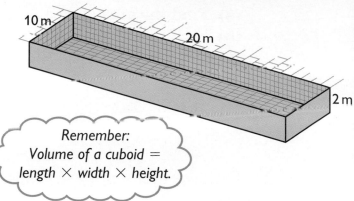

? **What shape is the
swimming pool?**

? **What is the volume of the
swimming pool?**

> Remember:
> Volume of a cuboid =
> length × width × height.

? **How many litres of water does the swimming
pool hold?**

> $1 m^3 = 1000$ litres

The bottom and sides of the pool are lined with tiles.

? **What area is tiled?**

Task

A new outdoor swimming pool is planned.

1 This is Design A.
   (a) What is the volume of
   the paddling section?
   (b) What is the volume of
   the swimming section?
   (c) How many litres of water does
   the whole pool hold?

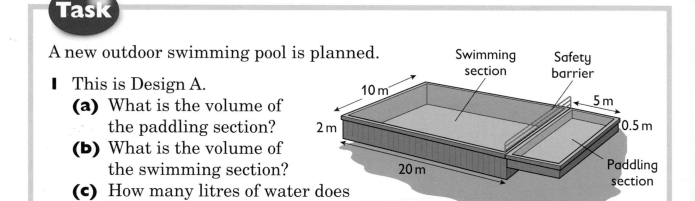

2 Make up your own design to put forward as Design B.
   Draw it and label it with its measurements.
   Work out how much water your pool holds.

? **How do you find the volume of this shape?**

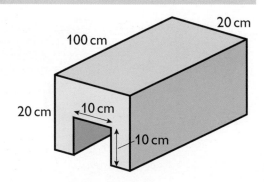

Exercise

1 Find the volume of each of these shapes.

(a)

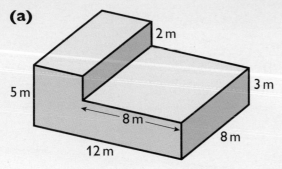

(b)

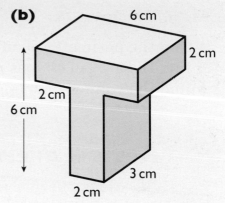

2 Look at Meena's new chicken shed.

(a) What is its volume?

(b) Each chicken needs $0.5\,m^3$ of space in the shed.
How many chickens can Meena have?

(c) Meena paints the outside of the shed (but not the roof) brown.
How many tins of paint does she buy?

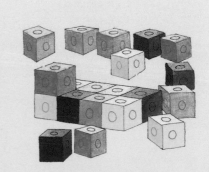

1 tin of paint covers $10\,m^2$.

Meena

Investigation

How many different cuboids can be made from 20 multilink cubes?

1 What is the volume of each cuboid?

2 What are the measurements of each cuboid?

3 Find the total surface area of each cuboid.

4 Which cuboid has the largest surface area?

Finishing off

Review exercise

1 This puzzle cube is made from centimetre cubes.
   (a) What is the volume of the
   puzzle cube?
   (b) What is the area of one face of the
   puzzle cube?
   (c) How many faces does the puzzle
   cube have?
   (d) What is the total surface area of
   the puzzle cube?

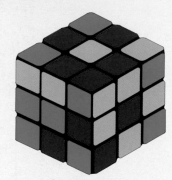

2 Mrs Green is buying fencing
   to go round her garden.
   (a) What is the perimeter of
   Mrs Green's garden?
   Fence panels are 2 m long.
   She already has a gate,
   2 m wide.
   (b) How many fence panels
   does she buy?

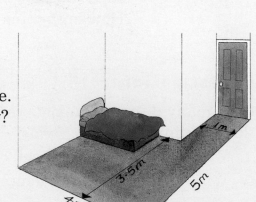

3 Mercy is buying carpet for her
   bedroom.
   Carpet is sold by the square metre.
   How much carpet does Mercy buy?

4 The perimeter of a square photograph
is 40 cm.

   (a) What is the length of one side of
the photograph?

   (b) What is the area of the photograph?

5 John has a new rug for his bedroom.

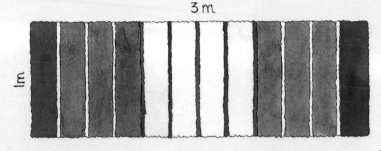

3 m

1 m

   (a) What is the area of the rug in m²?

m^2 means square metres.

   (b) What are the measurements of the
rug in **centimetres**?

cm^2 means square centimetres.

   (c) What is the area of the rug in cm²?

   (d) How many cm² make 1 m²?

Investigation

1 Collect a cereal packet and a matchbox.

2 Measure the length, width and height of both your boxes.

3 Find the volume of each box.

4 How many matchboxes can you fit into your cereal packet?

5 Find the surface area of each box.

I will cut up my cereal packet and make it into match boxes.

Michelle

How many match boxes can Michelle make?

18 Percentages

Review

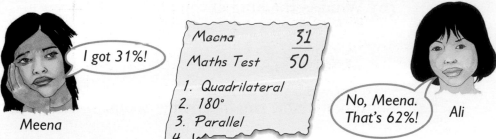

I got 31%!

Meena

Meena   31/50
Maths Test
1. Quadrilateral
2. 180°
3. Parallel
4.

No, Meena. That's 62%!

Ali

? **Who is right, Meena or Ali?**

Meena's mark is given as the fraction $\frac{31}{50}$. An equivalent fraction is $\frac{62}{100}$.

? **Explain why this is 62%.**

? **Change $\frac{3}{5}$ into a percentage.**

Task

Alan has done a test on percentages.

1 Mark it for him.

> **1** Convert these to percentages.
>
> **(a)** $\frac{1}{2}$ = 50% **(b)** $\frac{1}{10}$ = 10% **(c)** $\frac{2}{5}$ = 20%
>
> **(d)** $\frac{3}{5}$ = 30% **(e)** $\frac{3}{4}$ = 75%
>
> **2** Convert these to percentages.
> Cancel your answers as far as possible.
>
> **(a)** 80% = $\frac{80}{100}$ = $\frac{8}{10}$ = $\frac{4}{5}$ **(b)** 25% = $\frac{25}{100}$ = $\frac{5}{10}$ = $\frac{1}{2}$
>
> **(c)** 50% = $\frac{50}{100}$ = $\frac{5}{10}$ = $\frac{1}{2}$ **(d)** 20% = $\frac{20}{100}$ = $\frac{2}{10}$ = $\frac{1}{5}$
>
> **(e)** 35% = $\frac{35}{100}$ = $\frac{9}{20}$

2 Give his mark as a percentage.

Ali writes:

$\frac{18}{75} \times \frac{100}{100} = \frac{24}{100}$

so $\frac{18}{75}$ = 24%

? **Explain Ali's working.**

? **How do you write $\frac{8}{40}$ as a percentage?**

Exercise

1 Copy and complete the statements below.

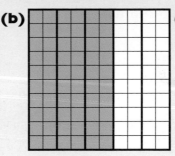

(a) $\dfrac{7}{10} = \dfrac{}{100}$

(b) $\dfrac{3}{5} = \dfrac{}{100}$

(c) $\dfrac{23}{100} = \dfrac{}{100}$

2 **(a)** Write these percentages as fractions out of 100.

(i) 40%   **(ii)** 25%   **(iii)** 35%

(iv) 60%   **(v)** 32%   **(vi)** 15%

(b) Cancel your answers to part **(a)** as far as possible.

3 Change these fractions to percentages.

(a) $\dfrac{1}{5}$ **(b)** $\dfrac{1}{10}$ **(c)** $\dfrac{9}{10}$

(d) $\dfrac{13}{20}$ **(e)** $\dfrac{11}{25}$ **(f)** $\dfrac{5}{8}$

4 Copy the crossword grid below.
Change the clues to percentages and write the answers in your grid.

Across

1 $\dfrac{1}{4}$ 2 $\dfrac{7}{10}$ 3 $\dfrac{1}{20}$ 4 $\dfrac{3}{5}$ 5 $\dfrac{2}{5}$

Down

1 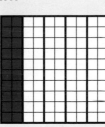   2 $\dfrac{3}{4}$ 3 $\dfrac{1}{2}$ 4 $\dfrac{120}{200}$

Working out percentages

In a TV show, viewers vote players off the programme.

> The person with the **most** votes leaves the programme!

BOBBY
28%

PHIL
190,000 votes
out of 500,000

LINDA
12%

RON

Phil's wife writes:

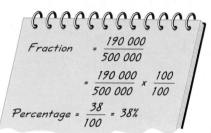

Fraction $= \dfrac{190\,000}{500\,000}$

$= \dfrac{190\,000}{500\,000} \times \dfrac{100}{100}$

Percentage $= \dfrac{38}{100} = 38\%$

? **Is she right?**

? **How can you work out the percentage that Ron has?**

? **Who leaves?**

Task

In another programme there were 300 000 votes.
Sui Lin has 14% of the votes. Clare has 75 000 votes.
Mike has 96 000 votes. Simon has the rest.

1 What percentage does each person have?
2 Copy and complete this bar chart to show the voting.

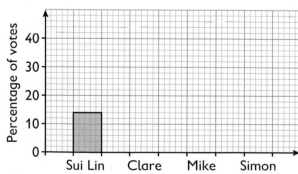

3 Who leaves?

? **How do you use your calculator to change this to a percentage?**
67 466 votes out of 213 500

Exercise

1 20% of the days in June 2003 were wet.
What percentage were dry?

2 30% of trains to London were late on Monday.
60% were on time.
What percentage of trains arrived early?

3 Change these to percentages.

(a) 150 out of 500   **(b)** 360 out of 600

(c) $\frac{4000}{8000}$ **(d)** $\frac{20}{80}$

(e) $\frac{12}{20}$ **(f)** $\frac{11}{55}$

(g) $\frac{120}{1000}$ **(h)** 60 out of 80

4 A sweet shop does a survey of 500 of its customers.
240 like Krisp Bars best.
31% like Minto Flakes best.
The rest like Chocolicks.
(a) What percentage like each?
(b) Which is the favourite?

5 A football club carries out a survey of 3000 football fans.
(a) 2460 wear club scarves. What percentage is this?
(b) 1620 wear club shirts. What percentage is this?

Activity   400 cat owners answered this question.

> What is your cat's favourite food?

Here are the results.

Food	Number	Percentage	Fraction
Yummi-Kat		22	
Kitti-Fish	92		
Feline Fabs			$\frac{1}{4}$
Tiddle's Tasties			
None of these	40		

1 Copy and complete the table.

2 Draw a bar chart to show the results.

Using percentages

In a sale there is 20% off all CDs and videos.
John buys a CD originally priced at £15.

He writes:

Reduction = 20% of £15

$$= \frac{20}{100} \times £15$$

$$= £3$$

 Explain what John has done.   **How much does he pay?**

Task

1 Meena goes to the sales with £100 to spend.
Copy and complete the table showing the sale price of these goods.

Item	Full cost	Percentage off	Reduction	Sale price
Shoes	£55	20%		
T-shirt	£25	20%		
Nightdress	£20	20%		
Mirror	£120	30%		
Skirt	£45	20%		

2 Meena wants to buy the mirror.
What else can she buy?

3 Meena does not buy the mirror.
Can she buy all the other items?

You need some shoes.

Meena's Mum

Humza works out the cost of some jeans.

I'll work it out on my calculator.

Humza

20% off marked price

Jeans £33

 Which buttons does he press?

Exercise

1 Find the following.
    (a) 20% of 400   **(b)** 40% of 300
    (c) 25% of 40 litres   **(d)** 50% of 6 km
    (e) 15% of 80 litres   **(f)** 30% of $500
    (g) 6% of £50   **(h)** 40% of 20 kg

2 A group of workers are given a 10% pay rise.
How much extra does each receive after the rise?
    (a) Sarah earns £5 an hour.
    (b) James carns £280 a week.
    (c) Henry earns £1200 a month.
    (d) Helen earns £15 000 a year.

3 Which of these is cheapest?

    (a)   **(b)**   **(c)**

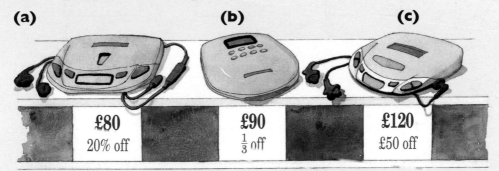

    £80   £90   £120
    20% off $\frac{1}{3}$ off   £50 off

4 A special pack of biscuits has an extra 20%.
The normal pack has 15 biscuits.
How many extra are there?

5 A holiday company offers 20% off these holidays.
    (a) 4 days in Jersey   £270
    (b) 2 days in Paris   £150
    (c) 3 days in Disneyland, Paris   £210
How much does each holiday cost now?

Activity   Value-added tax (VAT) is added to certain services.
                 VAT is charged at 17.5% of the original cost.
                 Use your calculator to work out the VAT on these items.

                 (a)   Garage bill   £207
                 (b)   Telephone bill   £164
                 (c)   Restaurant bill   £128

Finishing off

Now that you have finished this chapter you should be able to:

- convert percentages to fractions and fractions to percentages
- understand that the total amount is 100%
- work out a percentage of a quantity.

Review exercise

1. Look at these diagrams.

   (a) 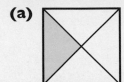 (b) 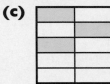 (c)   (d)

   For each one say
   (i) what fraction is shaded
   (ii) what percentage is shaded.

2. Change these fractions to percentages.

   (a) $\dfrac{1}{10}$ (b) $\dfrac{1}{4}$ (c) $\dfrac{1}{2}$ (d) $\dfrac{3}{4}$

   (e) $\dfrac{3}{10}$ (f) $\dfrac{9}{10}$ (g) $\dfrac{1}{5}$ (h) $\dfrac{4}{5}$

   (i) $\dfrac{9}{20}$ (j) $\dfrac{11}{25}$ (k) $\dfrac{17}{25}$ (l) $\dfrac{23}{50}$

3. Change these percentages to fractions.
   Cancel your answers as far as possible.

   (a) 50% (b) 25% (c) 75% (d) 10%

   (e) 46% (f) 76% (g) 4% (h) 5%

   (i) 90% (j) 45% (k) 85% (l) 22%

4. Which is the better sale?

   (a) (b)

5 Which of these is the cheapest?

(a)   **(b)**   **(c)**

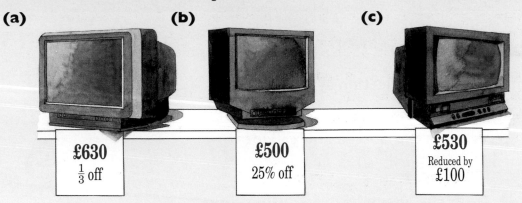

£630
$\frac{1}{3}$ off

£500
25% off

£530
Reduced by
£100

6 Tim has these marks.
Change them all to percentages.

History	$\frac{3}{5}$	Science	$\frac{14}{25}$	Maths	$\frac{7}{10}$
English	$\frac{40}{50}$	French	$\frac{13}{20}$	DT	$\frac{9}{10}$

In which subject has he done best?

7 **(a)** These items are in a '30% off' sale.
Work out how much each item is reduced by.

(i)   **(ii)**   **(iii)**

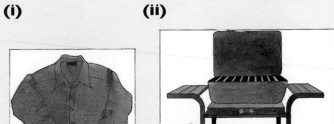

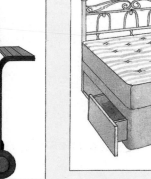

Was £30

Was £150

Was £350

(b) How much does each item cost in the sale?

Reflection

This shape has reflection symmetry.

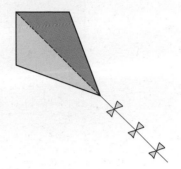

? **What is the dotted line called?**

? **Does the shape have any other lines of symmetry?**

Task

Make a snowflake design. This is how to do it.

1 Fold a square piece of coloured paper in half, then in half again.

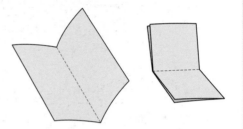

2 Cut out shapes along the fold lines.

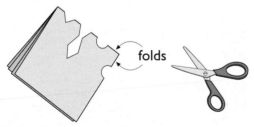

3 Unfold the paper.

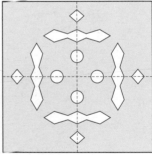

You will see a symmetrical pattern.

? **How many lines of symmetry does the pattern have?**

4 Now fold a piece of paper 3 times and cut out shapes along the folds.

? **How many lines of symmetry are there now?**

Make a poster about symmetry.
Decorate it with your snowflake designs.

 ? **How many lines of symmetry does a circle have?**

Exercise

SU

1. Copy each of these shapes and draw all the lines of symmetry for each one.

(a)   **(b)**   **(c)**

> *Only look at the shape. Don't worry about the picture.*

SU

2. Copy each of these shapes onto squared paper.
   Draw the reflections in the lines of symmetry.

(a)   **(b)**   **(c)**

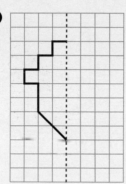
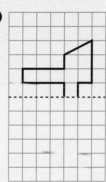
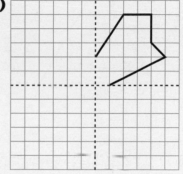

Activity   Design and colour a new logo for your local football team or youth club.
The logo must have reflection symmetry.
Decide how many lines of symmetry before you start.

Investigation

Look at this tennis court.

How many lines of symmetry does it have?

Investigate the symmetry of other sports pitches, such as a rugby pitch and a baseball park.

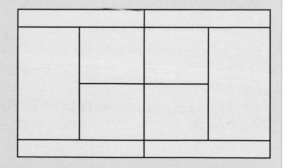

Rotation

This shape has rotation symmetry.

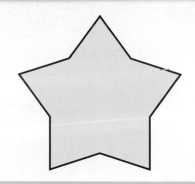

? **What is the order of rotation symmetry of the shape?**

? **Where is the centre of rotation of the shape?**

Task

1 Use a ruler and compasses to construct these flat shapes.

Reminder: Look at Chapter 7.

(a)

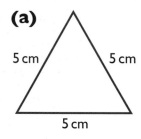

5 cm   5 cm

5 cm

(b)

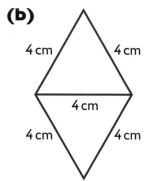

4 cm   4 cm

4 cm

4 cm   4 cm

(c)

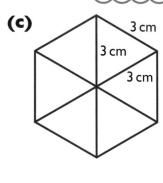

3 cm

3 cm

3 cm

2 Cut out your shapes carefully.
3 Fold each shape along each of its lines of symmetry.

? **Which angles in each shape are equal?**

? **Where do all the folds meet?**

4 Test each shape for rotation symmetry. Write down its order of rotation symmetry.
5 Glue your shapes into your book or onto a poster.
6 Write down the name of each shape and all the things you have found out about it.

? **Describe the symmetry of this shape.**

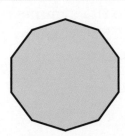

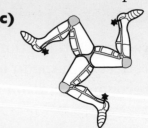

Exercise

1 What is the order of rotation symmetry of each of these shapes?

(a)

(b)

(c)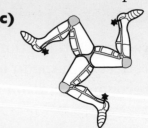

2 Copy these shapes and complete them so that they have the required symmetry.

(a) 1 line of symmetry
No rotation symmetry

(b) 4 lines of symmetry
Rotation symmetry
order 4.

(c) 2 lines of symmetry
Rotation symmetry
order 2.

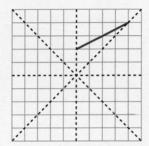

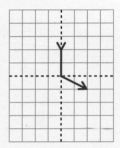

Activity Fold and cut a snowflake design which has reflection symmetry **and** rotation symmetry.

Reminder:
Look at the task on page 164.

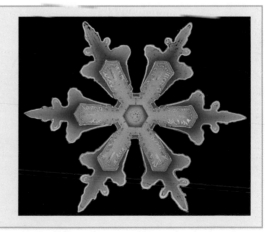

Finishing off

Now that you have finished this chapter you should be able to:

- recognise reflection symmetry and draw lines of symmetry
- reflect a shape in a line of symmetry
- recognise rotation symmetry and state its order.

Review exercise

1 **(a)** Which of these diagrams have reflection symmetry?
Draw the lines of symmetry.

(i)

(ii)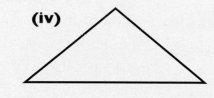

(iii)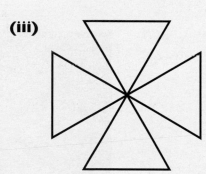

(iv)

(v)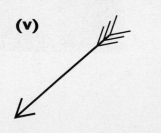

(vi)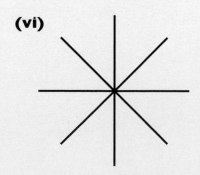

(b) Which of the diagrams have rotation symmetry?
State the order of symmetry.

(c) Which of the diagrams have reflection **and** rotation symmetry?

Activity This pattern was made using one shape, reflected and rotated to fit.

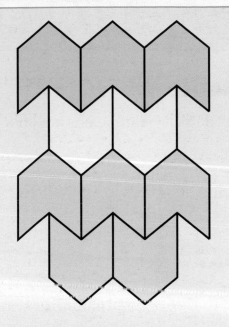

Here is how to make the shape.

1 Start with a square like this.

3 cm

3 cm

2 Add a shape to one side.

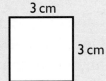

3 Take the same shape away from the opposite side.

4 Draw round the shape to make a pattern.

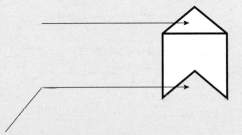

← Reflections

Rotations →

Design a shape of your own on card.

Cut the shape out carefully and draw round it to make a pattern using reflections and rotations.

20 Probability

Review

Probability can be shown on a probability scale.

? **What do these words mean?**
  (a) certain   **(b)** impossible   **(c)** evens

Task

1 Copy the probability scale below. Place the following events in the correct places on your scale.
  (a) The winning ticket will be an odd number.
  (b) The sun will set this evening.
  (c) An aeroplane will land on the school.
  (d) The temperature will go below 0 °C in December.
  (e) You will live to be 200.

| Impossible | Unlikely | Evens | Likely | Certain |

2 Add some more events to your scale.

Make sure you have something certain, something impossible and something that is evens.

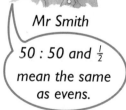

Mr Smith

50 : 50 and $\frac{1}{2}$ mean the same as evens.

3 What number means certain?
What number means impossible?

4 Add the numbers 0, $\frac{1}{2}$ and 1 to your probability scale.

? **Where do you place the terms very likely and very unlikely on your scale?**

? **Think of an event that is very likely and one that is very unlikely.**

Exercise

1 Use these words to describe the events below.

> certain   very likely   likely   evens
>
> unlikely   very unlikely   impossible

(a) Easter day will be in January.

(b) You will grow taller than your parents.

(c) The next person you meet will be female.

(d) You will live to be 50.

(e) A man will land on Mars sometime this century.

(f) A baby will be born somewhere in the world in the next 5 minutes.

(g) Someone will run a mile in less than 1 minute.

2 **(a)** Copy this table.

Probability				
0	Between 0 and $\frac{1}{2}$	$\frac{1}{2}$	Between $\frac{1}{2}$ and 1	1

(b) Write these events in the correct place in your table.
- You will score 6 with one throw of a die.
- A coin will land heads.
- The first card drawn from a pack will be a spade.
- It will rain tomorrow.
- You will throw an odd number with one throw of a die.
- You will throw a 9 with a normal die.

(c) Are any of the columns empty?
Put in some more events until you have 2 in each column.

Equally likely outcomes

Seven names are put in a hat to choose the captain of the tennis team.

| Wayne | Kim | Jack | Meena | Karl | Jo | Mark |

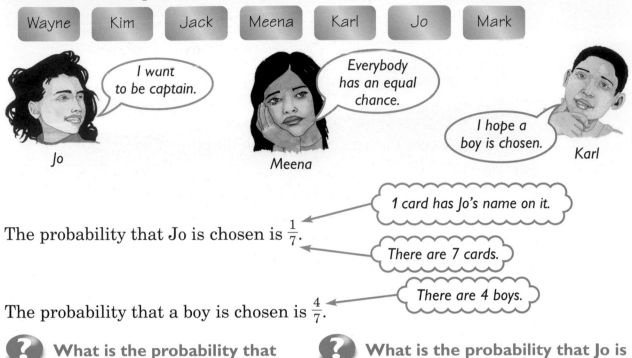

I want to be captain.

Jo

Everybody has an equal chance.

Meena

I hope a boy is chosen.

Karl

1 card has Jo's name on it.

The probability that Jo is chosen is $\frac{1}{7}$.

There are 7 cards.

There are 4 boys.

The probability that a boy is chosen is $\frac{4}{7}$.

? **What is the probability that a girl is chosen?**

? **What is the probability that Jo is not chosen?**

Task

Work with a friend and a pack of cards.
1 You shuffle the cards and your friend cuts the pack.
2 Look at your friend's card. Is it a spade, a heart, a diamond or a club?
3 Record the result in a copy of this table.
4 Return the card to the pack and repeat the experiment.
5 Keep going until you have 40 results.
6 Compare your results with the rest of the class.

Suit	Tally
Spade ♠	
Heart ♥	
Diamond ♦	
Club ♣	

This time your friend shuffles and you cut the pack.

? **Are you equally likely to get a spade, a heart, a diamond or a club?**

? **What is the probability of choosing a heart from your pack of cards?**

? **What is the probability of choosing a black card?**

Exercise

1 Decide if these events are equally likely or not equally likely.
   (a) A coin landing heads or tails.
   (b) A die landing 1, 2, 3, 4, 5 and 6.
   (c) Choosing a picture card or a numbered card from a pack.
   (d) A die landing on an odd number or an even number.

2 Pete and his friends cannot decide what to do on Saturday.
   They write these activities on cards and put them in a hat.

Pete draws out one of the cards.
Find the probability that the card shows
   (a) cinema
   (b) a sport
   (c) an activity that needs a ball.

3 Find the probability of each of these events.
   (a) You score 4 with one throw of a die.
   (b) This baby will be born on a Monday.
   (c) The next person you meet has a birthday
       in May or June.
   (d) You pick a spade from a pack of cards.

4 Megan is asked to draw a quadrilateral.
   She chooses one of these shapes at random.

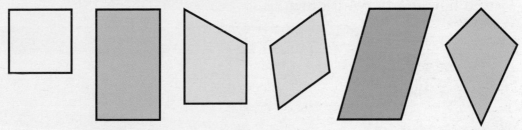

What is the probability that she draws
   (a) a square
   (b) a shape with 4 equal sides
   (c) a shape with 4 sides
   (d) a shape with parallel sides
   (e) a shape with 5 sides?

Estimating probability

Mercy is practising basketball.
She has 20 shots for a basket.

This table shows the outcomes.

Too high	5
Too low	7
A basket	8
Total	20

Mercy estimates the probability that she scores a basket.

Mercy

I **estimate** that the probability of my scoring a basket next shot is $\frac{8}{20}$.

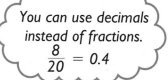

You can use decimals instead of fractions.
$\frac{8}{20} = 0.4$

  Estimate the probability that Mercy throws the ball too high with her next shot.

Task

1 Throw a drawing pin 50 times.

Point up   Point down

2 Use a copy of this table to record how many times it lands point up and how many point down.

	Tally	Frequency
Point up		
Point down		

  Is your drawing pin equally likely to land point up or point down?

  Estimate the probability that the drawing pin lands point down the next time you throw it.

  Are estimated probabilities accurate?

Exercise

1 Ali's bus arrives late 7 times in 10 days.

(a) Estimate the probability that the bus will arrive late the next day.

(b) How many times does the bus arrive on time in the 10 days?

(c) Estimate the probability that the bus will arrive on time the next day.

2 This is a record of the weather in Brightsea last June.

Weather	Frequency (number of days)
Sunny	12
Cloudy	15
Wet	3

(a) How many days are there in June?

(b) Estimate the probability that a day next June will be

(i) sunny   **(ii)** cloudy   **(iii)** wet.

3 Karl asks 100 people to choose their favourite holiday destination.

Holiday destination	Frequency
Spain	21
France	12
USA	9
Britain	27
Italy	16
Others	15

Estimate the probability that the next person asked will choose

(a) Spain   **(b)** Britain   **(c)** USA.

Activity   **1**   Work with a friend. Toss a coin 100 times.
Record your results in a table like this.

	Tally	Frequency
Heads		
Tails		

2 What fraction of the throws are heads?

3 Is the probability of a head $\frac{1}{2}$?

Finishing off

Now that you have finished this chapter you should be able to:

- mark events on a probability scale
- calculate probabilities using equally likely outcomes
- use an experiment to estimate probabilities.

Review exercise

1 For each of the events below, decide if it is certain, likely, evens,
   unlikely or impossible.
   (a) A lost shoe is for the right foot.
   (b) There will be a full moon this month.
   (c) You will make a snowman in April next year.
   (d) You will make a phone call next week.
   (e) The sun will not rise tomorrow.

2

	A	B	C	D	E	F
1			£1			50p
2	10p				20p	
3			10p			
4					20p	
5	50p		10p			20p
6						

Fortune squares

Pay 10p to roll the dice to choose a square.

Win the amount in that square.

(a) Tim plays the game.
He throws 2 and A.
Does he win any money?
(b) How many squares are there?
(c) How many winning squares are there?
(d) What is the probability of winning?
(e) What is the probability of winning
   (i) 10p **(ii)** 20p
   (iii) 50p **(iv)** £1?

3 Christina asks 100 people to choose a number from 1 to 10.
Here are the results.

Number	1	2	3	4	5	6	7	8	9	10
Frequency	5	10	8	10	9	10	25	10	9	4

(a) Are the numbers equally likely to be chosen?

(b) Estimate the probability that the next person will choose 1.

(c) Estimate the probability that the next person will choose 7.

(d) Ask the people in your class to choose a number from 1 to 10.
Estimate the probability for each number.

4

Congratulations

You are a prizewinner.
Return this ticket to claim your prize.

The prizes

5 prizes of £5   2 prizes of £20

1 prize of £50

(a) How many prizes are there?

(b) What is the probability you win £50?

(c) What is the probability you win £5?

(d) What is the probability you win more than £5?

5 Jack is a keen tennis player.
He serves 20 balls.
3 of these are out.

(a) Estimate the probability
that the next ball will be out.

(b) Estimate the probability
that the next ball will be in.

(c) Jack serves 40 more balls.
How many do you expect to
be out?
Explain your answer.

Sequences

Michelle and John play **Find the rule**.
Michelle writes down her sequence.

1st term	2nd term	3rd term	4th term	5th term
4	8	12	16	20

John has the correct rule.
He writes it down like this.

$term = 4 \times position.$ So $t = 4 \times p$

You multiply the position number by 4.

John

? **What is the 100th term in Michelle's sequence?**

John writes down his sequence.

1st term	2nd term	3rd term	4th term	5th term
5	6	7	8	9

Are you multiplying by 5?

Michelle

? **Michelle is wrong. How can you tell?**
What is John's rule?

Task

1 Write down the first 5 terms of these sequences.
   (a) $t = 5 \times p$ **(b)** $t = 6 \times p$ **(c)** $t = 7 \times p$
   Look at how the sequences increase. What do you notice?

2 Write down the rules for these sequences.
(a)	2	3	4	5	6
(b)	12	13	14	15	16
(c)	102	103	104	105	106

   Look at how the sequences increase. What do you notice?
   Write down the 100th term in each sequence.

3 Make up a sequence of your own. Ask a friend to find your rule.

? **What is the rule for this sequence?**
   1 4 9 16 25 36 49 64 81 100

Exercise

1 Find the next 3 terms of these sequences.

(a) 5   10   15   20

(b) 7   12   17   22

(c) 16   25   34   43

(d) 16   13   10   7

2 Write down the first 5 terms of the sequences with these rules.

(a) $t = 3 \times p$

(b) $t = 8 \times p$

(c) $t = p + 5$

(d) $t = p + 7$

3 Say whether Michelle has the right or the wrong rule for each sequence.

Michelle, can you find these rules?

Position, p,	1	2	3	4	5	
(a)	9	18	27	36	45	$t = 9 \times p$
(b)	10	19	28	37	46	$t = p + 9$
(c)	20	40	60	80	100	$t = 10 \times p$
(d)	11	12	13	14	15	$t = p + 10$

4 Find the rules for these sequences.

(a) 10   20   30   40   50

(b) 2   4   6   8   10

(c) 13   14   15   16   17

(d) 101   102   103   104   105

It may help you to copy these out and write position numbers above the sequence.

Activity Michelle thinks of a rule.
What is Michelle's rule?
Think of as many answers as you can.

The first number in my sequence is 4.

Looking for patterns

Stuart is using bricks to build stairs in his garden.
He adds bricks to make them higher, like this.

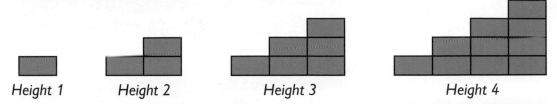

Height 1   Height 2   Height 3   Height 4

 Stuart builds stairs of height 4. He then makes them one step higher. How many more bricks does he use? Where does he put them?

Task

Investigate the number of bricks Stuart uses.

1 Copy and complete this table.

Height of stairs	1	2	3	4	5
Number of new bricks	1	2			
Total number of bricks	1				

2 Look at the numbers of bricks.
What patterns can you see?

3 How many bricks does he need for stairs of height 6?

4 Draw these stairs.
Count the number of bricks. Is your answer to part 3 correct?

5 Stuart has 30 bricks.
What are the highest stairs that Stuart can build?

Stuart now builds stairs of height 9.
He starts by laying 9 bricks on the ground.
Then he puts 8 bricks on top, then 7 and
so on.

> So far
> I have used
> 9 + 8 + 7 = 24
> bricks.

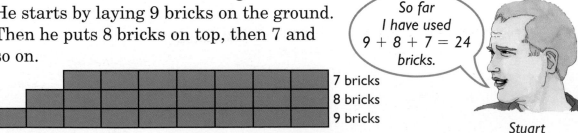

7 bricks
8 bricks
9 bricks

Stuart

6 How many bricks does he use altogether?

The total numbers of bricks used are called **triangular numbers**.

 Why do you think they are called triangular numbers?

Exercise

Lucy makes triangles with counters.

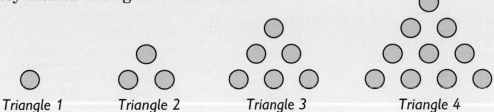

Triangle 1   Triangle 2   Triangle 3   Triangle 4

1 Draw the next triangle
for Lucy.

*Make the
triangles with counters
to help you.*

Lucy

2 **(a)** Draw a table to show the number of the counters for each
triangle.
  (b) Fill in the table.

3 **(a)** What patterns are there in the number of counters?
  (b) What type of numbers are they?

4 **(a)** How many counters does she use for triangle 7?
  (b) Draw triangle 7.
  (c) Count the number of counters.
Is your answer to part **(a)** correct?

5 How many counters does Lucy need for the 9th triangle?

6 **(a)** Lucy has 500 counters.
What is the largest triangle she can make?
  (b) How many counters does she have left over?

Activity

Look at this method to find the 10th triangular number.

$1 + 10 = 11$

$2 + 9 \ = 11$

$3 + 8 \ = 11$ $5 \times 11 = 55$ is the 10th triangular number

$4 + 7 \ = 11$

$5 + 6 \ = 11$

*The number 11
occurs 5 times.*

Use this method to find the 20th triangular number.

Flow charts

? **Put the number 3 into this flow chart.**
What are the outputs?

? **Look at the outputs.**
Which of these statements are true?

1 All the numbers are multiples of 3.

2 All the numbers are odd.

3 The difference between the numbers is always 3.

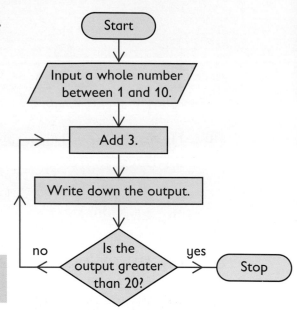

Start

Input a whole number between 1 and 10.

Add 3.

Write down the output.

Is the output greater than 20?

no

yes

Stop

Task

1 Input other numbers between 1 and 10.
Record your results in a table like the one below.
The first one has been done for you.

Input	Outputs	Statement 1	Statement 2	Statement 3
1	4, 7, 10, 13, 16, 19, 22	False	False	True
2				
3				
4				

2 Match each statement with one of the comments.

Always true   Sometimes true   Never true

? **Look at the statement which is sometimes true.**
When is it true?

Exercise

Look at this flow chart.

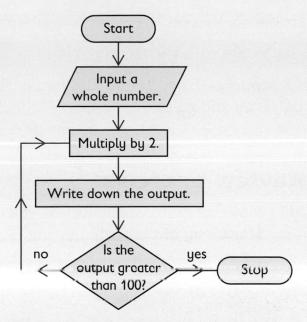

1. **(a)** Put the number 1 into the flow chart. Write down the outputs.
   (b) Which of these statements are true?

   > **A** The numbers are all even.   **B** The numbers are all powers of 2.

   > **C** The differences between the numbers are 2.

2. **(a)** Now put in the number 3. Write down the outputs.
   (b) Which of the statements are true?

3. Is Kim correct? Why?

4. One statement is never true. Which is it?

5. Look at this sequence.

   14   28   56   112   224

   What number did Kim input?

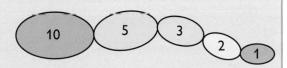

> Statement A is always true for any input.

Kim

6. **(a)** Kim inputs the number 5. Write down the outputs.
   (b) Write as many statements as you can about this sequence.

Activity

To get the number in the next segment of the caterpillar:
- for even numbers, divide by 2
- for odd numbers, add 1 then divide by 2
- stop when you get to 1.

10   5   3   2   1

Make some caterpillars of your own.
What do you notice?

Finishing off

Now that you have finished this chapter you should be able to:

- make a sequence from a rule, diagram or flow chart
- find patterns and rules.

Review exercise

1 Make as many sequences as you can from the numbers below. Make sequences with 5 terms.

1	3	5	6	10	15
21		20	25	9	16
8		2	32	12	4

2 Match each sequence to its rule.

$$t = 5 \times p \qquad t = p \times 3 \qquad t = p + 5 \qquad t = p + 3$$

(a) 3   6   9   12   15   **(b)** 4   5   6   7   8

(c) 6   7   8   9   10   **(d)** 5   10   15   20   25

3 This flow chart makes one of the sequences above. Which is it?

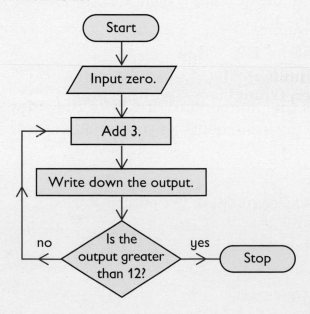

4 Some of these sequences are correct. In others one number is wrong.
Which sequences are correct?

(a) 6   10   14   18   22

(b) 20   17   13   10   7

(c) 1   2   4   8   10

(d) 2   −2   −6   −10   −14

5 Give the next 2 terms of the following sequences.

(a) A B C

(b) M T W T

(c) J F M A M

(d) point line triangle quadrilateral

(e) N NE E SE

(f) One hundred one thousand

Investigation

Look at these triangles.

  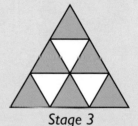

Stage 1   *Stage 2*   *Stage 3*

1 Draw the next 2 stages.

2 Copy and complete this table.

Stage number	Number of green triangles	Number of white triangles

3 Look at the patterns in the numbers of green and white triangles.
Write down as many patterns as you can.

4 (a) How many green triangles are there in stage 6?

(b) How many white triangles are there in stage 6?

(c) Draw the 6th stage and check your answers to parts **(a)** and **(b)**.

5 Work out the **total** number of triangles for the 10th stage. (Do not draw it.)

Mrs Green

Try playing **Match my number** *with a friend. Hide your calculators from one another.*

Match my number

Jo and Christina are playing **Match my number** on calculators.

I put this number in my calculator.

406.38

Jo

My card says 932.13. It goes in my calculator.

932.13

Christina

I have 4 hundreds. Can you make your hundreds the same as mine?

I can take off 500 or add 500. Both will work.

406.38

C = ÷ ×

Jo's calculator

432.13

C = ÷ ×

Christina's calculator

 Has Christina added 500 or subtracted 500?

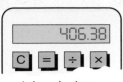

Jo's calculator

Christina's calculator

I have 3 hundreths. Can you match it?

Christina

? What does Jo subtract to make 3 hundredths?

I have no tens. Match me!

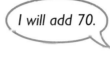

I will add 70.

? Christina adds 70.
What new number does she have on her calculator?

? What has happened to her hundreds?

? Jo has to match Christina's hundreds.
What does she do?

Jo's calculator

Christina's calculator

? Can they now match each other's numbers in two moves?

Play **Match my number** with a friend.
Keep asking questions until your numbers match.

Review

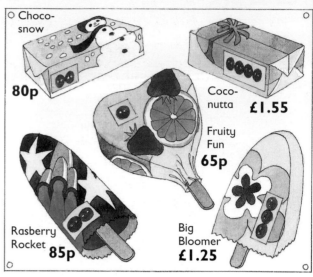

3 Coco-nuttas and 3 Raspberry Rockets please.

Megan

How much is that?

Samir

Choco-snow **80p**

Coco-nutta **£1.55**

Fruity Fun **65p**

Rasberry Rocket **85p**

Big Bloomer **£1.25**

Megan and Samir both work out the cost.

Megan writes:

	Cost each	×3
Coco-nutta	£1.55	£4.65
Raspberry Rocket	85p	
	Total	

Samir writes:

$3 \times (£155 + 85p)$

$= 3 \times £()$

$=$

Work out inside the brackets first.

? **What are Megan's and Samir's missing numbers?**

Task

Jo and 5 friends have £6 to spend on ice-creams.

1 Find different ways to buy 6 ice-creams with £6.

2 They are collecting the tokens ●● from the wrappers. Which way gets most tokens?

It will help if you make a table of prices first.

 You are working out the area of this shape. How can brackets help you?

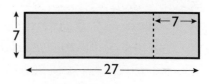

7

27

7

Exercise

1 Use brackets to work out these costs.
 (a) 2 each of peaches and pineapple rings.
 (b) 3 each of sugar and raisins.
 (c) 4 each of yoghurt and sugar.
 (d) 2 each of sugar, peaches and yoghurt.

Peaches 47p
Pineapple rings 53p
Raisins £1.35
Sugar 64p
Yoghurt £1.23

2 Use your calculator to work out these costs
 (a) 3 beans + 2 spaghetti
 (b) 4 plum tomatoes + 4 corned beef
 (c) 2 packs of sausages
   + 3 plum tomatoes + 1 soup
 (d) 3 beans + 3 packs of sausages
   + 3 corned beef.

Beans 33p
Soup 64p
Spaghetti 25p
Plum tomatoes 40p
Corned beef 70p
Sausages 61p

3 Look at this array of dots.
 There are 16 columns and 14 rows.
 You are going to work out 16 × 14.
 (a) (10×10) **(b)** (6×10)
 (c) (10×4) **(d)** (6×4)
 (e) 16×14

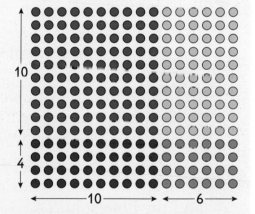

4 Work out these.
 Are the pairs the same?
 (a) (i) $(15 - 4) \times 2$
    (ii) $15 - (4 \times 2)$
 (b) (i) $(20 \times 4) \div 2$
    (ii) $20 \times (4 \div 2)$

Activity

Look at these 48 faces. There are 8 columns.
Each column has 4 blue faces and 2 green
faces. So $(4 + 2) \times 8 = 48$
 1 Look carefully at the faces.
  Write two more equations for this array.
 2 Draw a group of 36 faces.
  Ask a friend to write three equations for your faces.

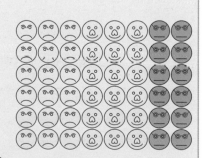

Tests of divisibility

? **What is the difference between an odd number and an even number?**

Look at these numbers.

92   18   60
24   181   216   35
17   134

? **Which of these numbers are divisible by 2, 5 or 10?
How can you tell?**

? **What is special about the numbers 3, 6, 9, 12, 15 …?
Continue the sequence.**

? **The digit total of 75 is 7 + 5 = 12.
What is the digit total of 96?**

Task

1 Copy this number grid.
2 **(a)** Find the digit totals of the numbers in the yellow squares.
   (b) Find the other numbers with the same digit total. Colour those squares yellow.
3 Now do the same for the green and the blue squares.
4 Colour the squares with digit totals of 12, 15 and 18.
5 What number divides into all the coloured numbers?

0	1	2	3	4	5	6	7	8	9
10	11	12	13	14	15	16	17	18	19
20	21	22	23	24	25	26	27	28	29
30	31	32	33	34	35	36	37	38	39
40	41	42	43	44	45	46	47	48	49
50	51	52	53	54	55	56	57	58	59
60	61	62	63	64	65	66	67	68	69
70	71	72	73	74	75	76	77	78	79
80	81	82	83	84	85	86	87	88	89
90	91	92	93	94	95	96	97	98	99

? **How can you tell if a number is divisible by 3?**

? **Which of these numbers are divisible by 3?**

123   345   750   507
234   456   570   705

Exercise

1 Find the digit totals of the numbers below.
List the numbers that are multiples of 3.

(a) 107, 207, 307, 407, 507

(b) 3003, 3004, 3005, 3006, 3007

(c) 5209, 5210, 5211, 5212, 5213, 5214

(d) 253, 263, 273, 283, 293, 303

2 **(a)** Copy this diagram.

(b) Sort all the numbers from 50 to 100

(c) Make a list of the numbers in the intersection.

(d) What can you say about the numbers in the intersection?

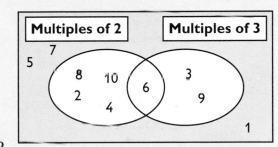

The overlap is called the intersection.

3 **(a)** Copy this diagram.

(b) Sort all the numbers from 11 to 50.

(c) List all the numbers in the intersection.

(d) What can you say about the numbers in the intersection?

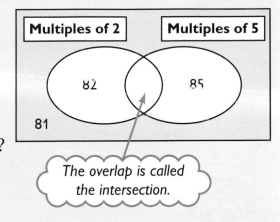

4 **(a)** Copy this table.

Multiples of 2	Multiples of 3	Multiples of 4

(b) Put these numbers in the correct columns.

 606   350   215   3000   3678   5375   249

(c) Fill in any empty spaces with 3-digit numbers.

Remainders

Pete and 4 friends go on the Tees Queen.

We'll share the cost between the 5 of us.

Pete

Group booking
TEES QUEEN CRUISE AND DISCO

4 hours of fun, food and fine countryside

Prices

Family ticket **£72.20**

Groups of 5 to 8 **£86.44**

Pete writes

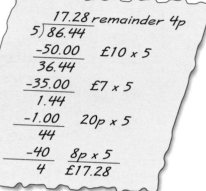

17.28 remainder 4p
5) 86.44
−50.00   £10 × 5
36.44
−35.00   £7 × 5
1.44
−1.00   20p × 5
44
−40   8p × 5
4   £17.28

? **Explain Pete's working.**

? **Who pays the 4p remainder?**

Mercy's calculator

? **Mercy uses a calculator.**
Explain Mercy's calculator display.

Task

1 Copy and complete this table of costs for Pete's trip.

Next week, Pete and 5 friends do the same trip.
The taxi and the party pack cost the same.
They need an extra meal.

Item	Cost	Cost per person	Remainder
Cruise	£86.44	£17.28	4p
Taxi	£10.34		
Food	£45.00		
Party pack	£11.52		
Total			

2 Complete a table of costs for 6 people.

? **Mercy uses her calculator to work out £86.44 ÷ 6.**
Her calculator says 14.406 667.
What does this mean?

Exercise

1 Work these out.
Give your answer as a whole number and a remainder.
(a) $373 \div 5$ **(b)** $233 \div 4$ **(c)** $290 \div 3$ **(d)** $187 \div 4$
(e) $217 \div 6$ **(f)** $288 \div 5$ **(g)** $843 \div 6$ **(h)** $371 \div 3$

2 Make a sensible decision about the answers to these problems.
(a) Skating costs £4. I have £30.
How many tickets can I buy?
(b) Mr Smith needs 30 cans for a school trip.
How many packs of 4 does he buy?
(c) A baker makes 30 cakes.
How many packs of 4 does he make?
(d) 30 people are coming to Alan's party.
Doughnuts are on special offer.
How many packs does he buy?

 3 Look at this diagram. There are 28 circles.
(a) You have 2 colours.
You colour the same number of circles
in each colour.
How many circles are left white?
(b) How many circles are left white when you use
3, 4, 5, 6, 7 and 8 colours?

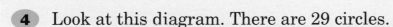

 4 Look at this diagram. There are 29 circles.
(a) You have 2 colours.
You colour the same number of
circles in each colour.
How many circles are left white?
(b) How many circles are left white when you use
3, 4, 5, 6, 7 and 8 colours?

Activity Complete this statement in as many ways as you can.

$38 \div$ ▨ $=$ ▨ remainder 2

Draw a diagram to show each one.

Number puzzles

Look at this **Magic square**.

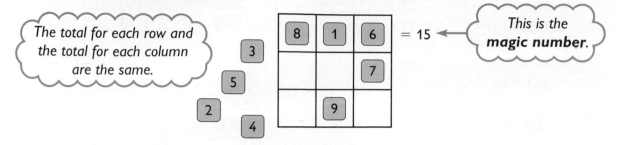

The total for each row and the total for each column are the same.

= 15

This is the **magic number**.

? **What numbers go in the empty spaces?**

? **What is the total of each diagonal line?**

Task

1 **(a)** Look at this magic square.
 (b) What is the magic number?
 (c) Fill in the missing numbers.

2 **(a)** Now add 3 to every number.
 (b) Is it still a magic square?
 (c) What is the new magic number?
 (d) Add a different number.
  What happens to the magic number?

3 **(a)** Subtract 2 from every number.
 (b) Is it still a magic number?
 (c) What is the new magic number?
 (d) Subtract a different number.
  What happens to the magic number?

4 **(a)** Now multiply each number by 2.
 (b) Is it still a magic square?
 (c) What happens to the magic number?

? **You add the same number to all the numbers in a magic square.
What happens to the magic number?**

Exercise

1 Look at this magic square.

(a) What is the magic number?

(b) Complete the magic square.

(c) Make a new magic square by doubling each number.
What is the new magic number?

(d) Make two more magic squares using × 3 and × 5.

(e) What happens to the magic number each time?

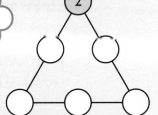

2 Look at this puzzle.
The total for each line of three numbers is 11.

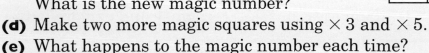
11 is the target number.

(a) Complete the puzzle using these numbers.

(b) Make a different puzzle by multiplying each number by 3.

(c) What happens to the target number?

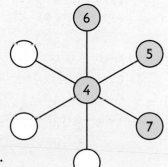

3 Look at this puzzle.
The target number is 12.

(a) Complete the puzzle.

(b) Use these numbers to make a new puzzle.

 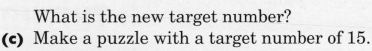

What is the new target number?

(c) Make a puzzle with a target number of 15.

Activity Look at this target board.
The target number is in the centre.
Choose 1 or more red numbers and 1
or more blue numbers.
Connect your numbers with +, −, ×, ÷
and brackets to make the target number.
One way is (6 × 4) + (5 − 1) = 28.
Find 5 more ways to reach the target.

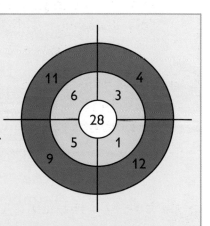

Finishing off

Now that you have finished this chapter you should be able to:

- use brackets
- apply tests of divisibility by 2, 3, 5 and 10
- know about remainders
- solve some mathematical puzzles, recognise and explain patterns.

Review exercise

1 Work out these. Which pairs have the same answers?

(a) (i) $(4 \times 3) + (4 \times 2)$ (ii) $4 \times (3 + 2)$

(b) (i) $(5 + 3) \times 2$ (ii) $(5 \times 2) + (3 \times 2)$

(c) (i) $(6 - 4) \times 5$ (ii) $(6 - 5) \times 4$

(d) (i) $(13 \times 3) + 1$ (ii) $(10 \times 3) + (3 \times 3) + 1$

2 Which is bigger?

(a) $(4 \times 5) + 3$ or $4 \times (5 + 3)$

(b) $(6 + 7) \times 3$ or $6 + (7 \times 3)$

(c) $20 \div (4 + 1)$ or $(20 \div 4) + 1$

(d) $(3 \times 4) \div 2$ or $3 \times (4 \div 2)$

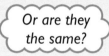

Or are they the same?

3 What is the cost of tickets for

(a) two adults and three children

(b) three adults and two children?

The Theatre Royal
presents
THE HOBBIT
Adults £8   Children £5.50

4 136 Year 8 students buy tickets for the Christmas Party.
Party poppers are sold in packs of 25.
How many packs are needed?

SU

5 (a) Copy this diagram.

(b) Sort all the numbers between 10 and 50.

(c) List all the numbers in the intersection.

(d) What can you say about the numbers in the intersection?

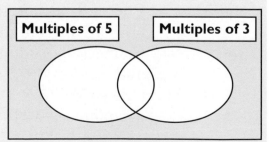

Multiples of 5   Multiples of 3

SU

6 **(a)** Copy this table.

(b) Put these numbers in the correct columns.

236 333 105
140 173 2000
19 3000 463
2811 91 844
723 3245

	Divisible by			
2	**3**	**5**	**10**	**Other**

7 Work these out.

Give each answer as a whole number and a remainder, if there is one.

(a) **(i)** $66 \div 6$ **(ii)** $67 \div 6$

     (iii) $72 \div 6$ **(iv)** $76 \div 6$

(b) **(i)** $36 \div 6$ **(ii)** $38 \div 6$

     (iii) $360 \div 6$ **(iv)** $365 \div 6$

(c) **(i)** £42.00 $\div 6$ **(ii)** £42.54 $\div 6$

     (iii) £42.58 $\div 6$ **(iv)** £42.53 $\div 6$

Activity

Look at this target board.
The target number is in the centre.
Choose 1 or more red numbers and 1 or more blue numbers.
Connect your numbers with $+, -, \times, \div$ and brackets to make the target number.
Find 8 more ways to reach the target.

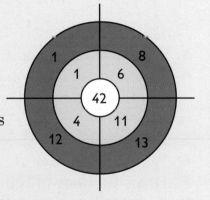

Investigation

SU

Look at this puzzle.
The target number is 24.

(a) Find the missing numbers.

(b) Copy the puzzle.
Multiply every number by 5.
What happens to the target number?

(c) Investigate what happens to the target number if you multiply all the numbers by

     (i) 2   **(ii)** 3   **(iii)** 4.

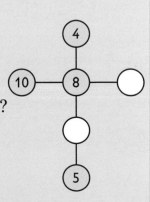

Reflections and rotations

This pattern is made by rotating a kite
4 times round point P.
Each rotation is a quarter turn.
The pattern has rotation symmetry.

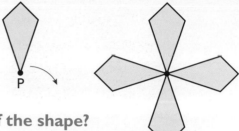

? **What is the order of rotation symmetry of the shape?**

The pattern also has reflection symmetry.

? **How many lines of symmetry does it have?**

Task

1 Draw a circle with a radius of 5 cm.
2 Use a ruler and protractor to construct this triangle
   inside the circle.

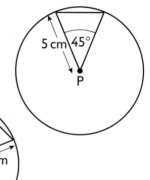

3 Construct a second triangle like this.
4 Now continue to construct triangles
   round point P, until you are back to
   the start.
5 Describe the finished shape.
6 What is its order of rotation symmetry?
7 Draw its lines of reflection symmetry.
8 Construct new shapes using
   angles of 30° and 60°.

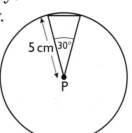

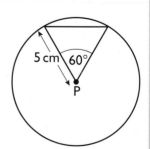

? **What happens when you use an angle of 80°?**

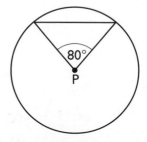

Exercise

1 A die has six faces.

(a) Copy each face and draw all the lines of symmetry.

(b) Describe the rotation symmetry of each face.

2 A football pitch has **two** lines of symmetry.
This diagram shows part of the markings on a football pitch.

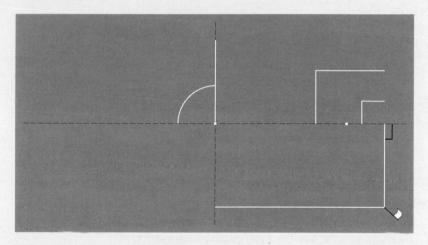

(a) Copy and complete the diagram.
(b) Describe the symmetry of the pitch.

Activity On a computer, use LOGO to draw shapes that have both reflection **and** rotation symmetry.

Describe the symmetry of each shape you draw.

Translations

In this computer game, the rescue helicopter, P, picks up survivors in the sea.

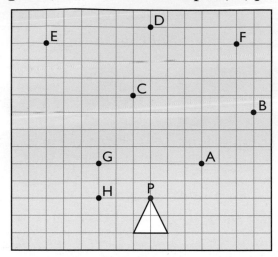

To move the helicopter Humza uses the arrow keys.

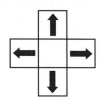

I'm going to rescue A first.

Humza

Humza moves the helicopter to survivor A.
The helicopter goes to the right and up.

 How far does it move to the right? How far up?

The move is called a **translation** of
3 to the right and 2 up.

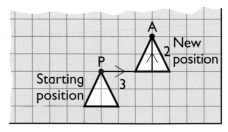

Task

Complete the rescue mission to pick up all the survivors in order.

Describe each translation like this.

    P to A, 3 right, 2 up.
    A to B, _____ .

 In a translation, which of these change: shape, size, position?

Exercise

1 On this grid, shape A is translated 5 left and 2 up.

(a) Copy the grid.

(b) Draw shape A in its new position. Label it B.

(c) Translate shape B 4 right and 2 up. Draw shape B in its new position. Label it C.

(d) What single translation takes shape C back to shape A?

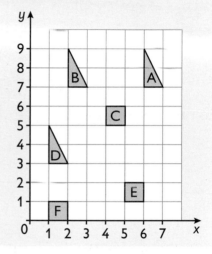

2 Look at this grid.
Describe each of these translations.

(a) A to D   (b) B to A

(c) E to C   (d) C to E

(e) F to E   (f) D to B

Why is A to C impossible?

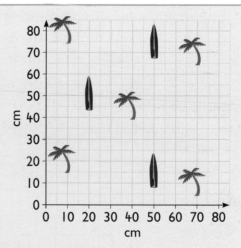

Activity (a) Look at this wallpaper. How many basic patterns are there?
Use translations to describe the repeating patterns in the design.

(b) Design some wallpaper of your own that has a repating pattern.

Activity On squared paper, design a computer game that uses translations.
Write down the translations needed to win the game.
Try the game out on a friend.

Finishing off

Now that you have finished this chapter you should be able to:

- recognise rotations, reflections and translations
- rotate, reflect and translate simple shapes.

Review exercise

1 The 50p coin has seven edges.
   (a) Draw the outline of the coin and all its lines of symmetry.
   (b) What is its order of rotation symmetry?

   In the middle of a 20p coin is a Tudor rose.
   (c) Describe the symmetry of the Tudor rose.

2 Look at the shapes on this grid.
   (a) Which shape is a translation of A? Describe the translation.
   (b) Which shape is a rotation of A? Describe the rotation.
   (c) Which shape is a reflection of A?

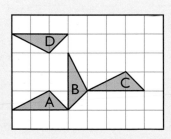

3 These are numbers in a calculator display.

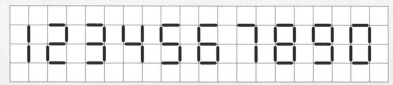

Copy the numbers and describe the symmetry (if any) of each.

SU

4 Copy this grid. Fill in the grid with the answers to the clues.
When you have finished, the green squares will give the name of
a shape that has reflection and rotation symmetry.
What is it?

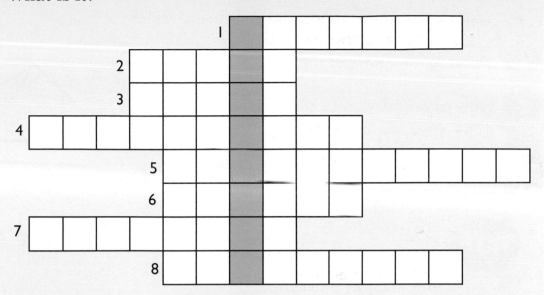

Clues
1 This shape has six sides.
2 A square has rotation symmetry of _____ 4.
3 A square is a four-sided _____.
4 Use a mirror for this.
5 This moves a shape to a new position.
6 You measure these with a protractor.
7 A turn.
8 To draw a shape accurately.

Nets

Look at this picture.

? **What is the name of the shape?**

? **How many faces does the shape have?**

? **How many vertices does the shape have?**

? **How many edges does the shape have?**

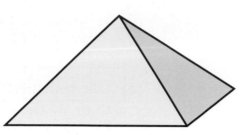

Task

You are going to make a pyramid.
Look at this **net** of a pyramid.

1 Make a full-size drawing of the net.

2 Decide where you need flaps.
   Draw the flaps.

3 Cut out the net with its flaps.

4 Fold the net and glue the edges to
   make a pyramid.

5 Now work with your friends and
   their pyramids.

   What shapes can you make with
   (a) 2   **(b)** 4   **(c)** 6   **(d)** 12 pyramids?

Save your pyramid for a later lesson.

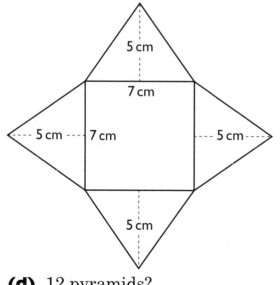

? **Which countries in the world are famous for pyramids?**

Exercise

1 **(a)** Use centimetre-squared paper to draw the net for a box of tissues.
Make it half the size of the real one.
(b) Add flaps and cut out the net.
(c) Construct the box.
(d) What is the name of this shape?

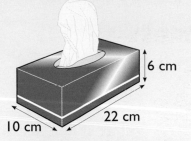

6 cm
22 cm
10 cm

2 **(a)** Use centimetre-squared paper to draw the net for this tool box. Choose your own scale.
(b) Add flaps and cut out the net.
(c) Construct the tool box.

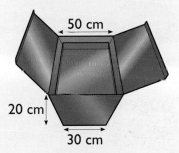

50 cm
20 cm
30 cm

3 **(a)** Use centimetre-squared paper to draw the net for this picnic basket.
Choose your own scale.
(b) Add flaps and cut out the net.
(c) Construct the picnic basket.

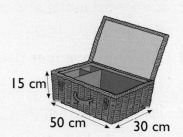

15 cm
50 cm
30 cm

Activity

1 Measure, in centimetres, an item of luggage.

2 Decide on a scale.

3 Draw a net for your item of luggage.

4 Add flaps and cut out the net.

5 Construct the case.

Some cases have wheels.

6 Make some and add them to the model.

7 Look at your friends' models.
How many different shapes are there?

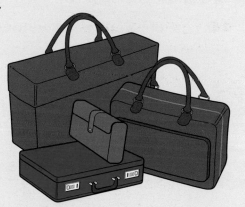

Drawing solid shapes

Look at this picture.

 What shape are the dice?

Task

For this task, you will need a die.

This cube is drawn on **isometric paper**.

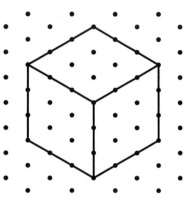

1 Copy the diagram onto isometric paper.

2 Look at your die.
Choose 3 sides and mark on the spots of the
die on your cube.

3 How many edges does a cube have?

4 How many edges can you see in the diagram?

5 Draw in the hidden edges using dashed lines.

6 Turn the die so that you see 3 different numbers.

7 Draw the diagram again with the new numbers.
Remember to draw the hidden lines.

8 Now draw a net of a die.

9 Mark the spots on the faces.

10 Cut out your net and make the die.

 **Look at the lines in your drawing.
In how many different directions do the lines run?**

 How many dimensions does your die have?

*In a real cube, the different
directions are all at right angles.*

 How many faces does your die have?

Exercise

1 Look at this shape.
  (a) What is its name?
  (b) In how many different directions do the lines run?
  (c) Are they at right angles?
  (d) How many dimensions does the shape have?

2 Draw these shapes on isometric paper. Remember to draw in the hidden lines.

(a)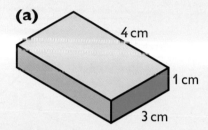
4 cm
1 cm
3 cm

(b)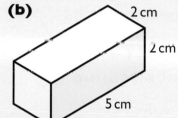
2 cm
2 cm
5 cm

(c)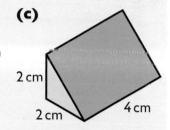
2 cm
2 cm
2 cm
4 cm

3 Are these flat or solid?
  (a) a triangle   **(b)** a Toblerone
  (c) a pyramid   **(d)** a samosa
  (e) a circle   **(f)** a pancake
  (g) a pizza   **(h)** a can of soup
  (i) a watermelon   **(j)** a square
  (k) an After Eight mint   **(l)** a carton of juice

Investigation

Copy and complete this table.

Name of shape	Number of sides or edges	Number of dimensions	Example
Line	1	1	————
Square	4	2	
Rectangle	4		
Cube			
Cuboid			
Pentagon			
Hexagon			

Plans and elevations

Look at the pyramid you made in the task on page 204.
Number the triangular faces.
Now place your pyramid on your desk.

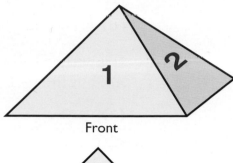

? **From how many different directions can you view it?**

? **Are all the views the same?**

Here is the view from the front.
This is called the front **elevation**.

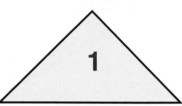

? **Where do you view from to see the right-side elevation? What about the back elevation?**

Task

1 Draw the right-side elevation.
   Mark the number on it.

2 Draw the left-side and rear elevations.
   Mark the numbers on them.

This is another view of the pyramid.
This is called the **plan**.

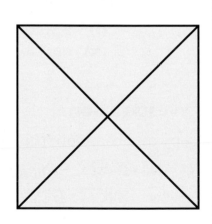

? **From which direction is this view?**

3 Draw the plan.
   Mark the numbers on it.

? **Look at this shape. What is it called?**

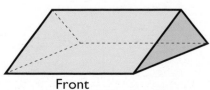

Front

? **What do the elevations and the plan look like?**

Exercise

1 Sophie, Pete, Christina, Jack and Megan see a ship at sea from different directions.

Who sees these views?

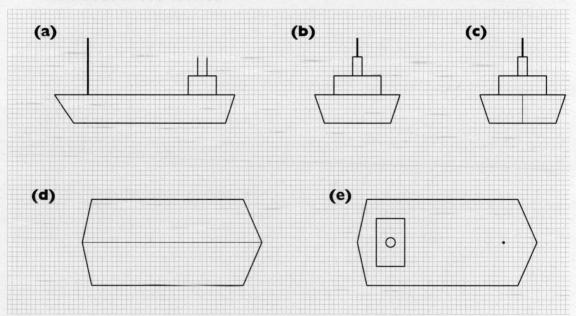

(a) **(b)** **(c)**

(d) **(e)**

2 Copy the diagrams and label the different views.

Activity **1** Draw the front and side elevations of one building of your school.

2 Draw the plan of the same building.

Finishing off

Now that you have finished this chapter you should be able to:

- draw nets and construct models
- draw plans and elevations
- use isometric paper.

Review exercise

1   Stuart and Mary see this famous
building on holiday.
Mary views it from the ground.
Stuart goes on a helicopter ride.

(a)

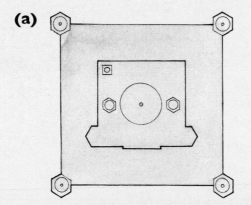

(b)

(i)   Who sees this view?   **(i)**   Who sees this view?
(ii) What is this view called? **(ii)** What is this view called?
(c) What is the name of the building?
(d) Which country did Stuart and Mary visit?

2   **(a)** Draw 2 different nets for this cube.
    (b) Make one cube.
    (c) Write on the letters you can see here.
    (d) How many faces can you not see?
    (e) Choose letters for the hidden faces and
    write them on.

3 Jo, Kim, Lucy and Meena go camping.
They view their tent from different
directions.
It only has one window.

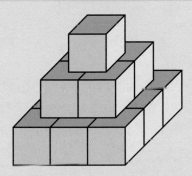

 (a) Jo sees the front elevation.
  Which view does she see?
 (b) Kim sees the rear elevation.
  Which view does she see?
 (c) Lucy sees the side elevation without windows.
  Which view does she see?
 (d) Which view does Meena see?

 (i) **(ii)** **(iii)**   **(iv)**

  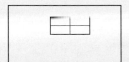 

 (e) Draw a plan view of the tent.

Investigation

Ali is making pyramids from 5 cm cubes.

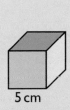

5 cm

1 How does she build a pyramid from 5 cubes?
2 How does she build a pyramid from 14 cubes?
3 How does she build a pyramid from 30 cubes? What do you notice?
4 How many cubes does she need for the next size of pyramid?
5 Copy and complete this table.

Level of pyramid	Number of cubes needed	Area of base
1	1	25 cm²
2	$(2 \times 2) + 1 = 5$	100 cm²
3	$(3 \times 3) +$ level 2 = 14	
4		
5		
6		

Plotting co-ordinates

Kim and Harry are playing **Starships**.
Here is Kim's grid.
They take it in turns to guess a point.

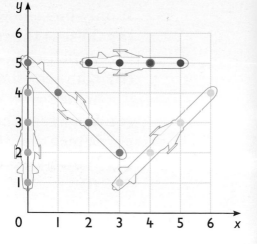

? **Harry guesses the point (3, 2). Is this a hit?**

The winner is the first person to find all the complete starships.

Harry finds one of Kim's starship.
He writes down the co-ordinates.

Look the x and y co-ordinates always add up to 5.

(0, 5)
(1, 4)
(2, 3)
(3, 2)

Harry

Task

1 Write down the co-ordinates of Kim's starships.
2 What patterns do you notice?
3 Which of these sets of co-ordinates make starships?

A (1, 2)	B (0, 4)	C (1, 1)	D (2, 3)
(1, 3)	(1, 3)	(2, 2)	(3, 3)
(1, 4)	(2, 2)	(3, 5)	(4, 3)
(1, 5)	(3, 1)	(4, 2)	(5, 3)

4 Kim gets hits at (2, 3) and (2, 6).
What other points should she try?
What is the pattern for this starship?
5 Play your own game of **Starships** with a friend.
What patterns do you notice in the starships?

When points lie on a straight line the co-ordinates have a pattern.

? **Is Kim right?**

Kim

Exercise

1 **(a)** Write down the co-ordinates of the points marked on each of these lines.

(i)

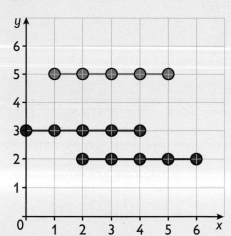

(ii)

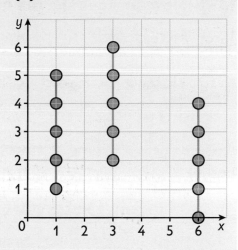

(b) What patterns do you notice when the lines are
   (i) horizontal
   (ii) vertical?

(c) Which of these sets of points make horizontal lines?
   (i) (2, 4), (3, 4), (4, 5), (5, 6)
   (ii) (3, 7), (4, 7), (5, 7), (6, 7)

(d) Which of these sets of points make vertical lines?
   (i) (1, 3), (1, 4), (1, 5), (1, 6)
   (ii) (3, 4), (3, 5), (4, 3), (5, 3)

2 **(a)** Draw a pair of axes from 0 to 8.

(b) Plot these points.

   (2, 6), (3, 5), (4, 4), (5, 3)

(c) Do they make a straight line?

(d) What patterns do you notice?

3 **(a)** Draw a pair of axes from 0 to 8.

(b) Plot these points.

   (8, 6), (7, 5), (6, 4), (5, 3)

(c) Do they make a straight line?

(d) What patterns do you notice?

Plotting a formula

Lucy is training for a marathon. She runs at 10 kilometres per hour.

How far does she run in 3 hours?

Lucy writes:

Distance = Speed × Time
My speed is 10 km per hour so: Distance = 10 × Time

Time (hours)	0	1	2	3	4	5
Time × 10	0	10	20			
Distance (km)	0	10	20			

Explain Lucy's working.

Look at Lucy's graph.
Why has she plotted the points (1, 10) and (2, 20)?

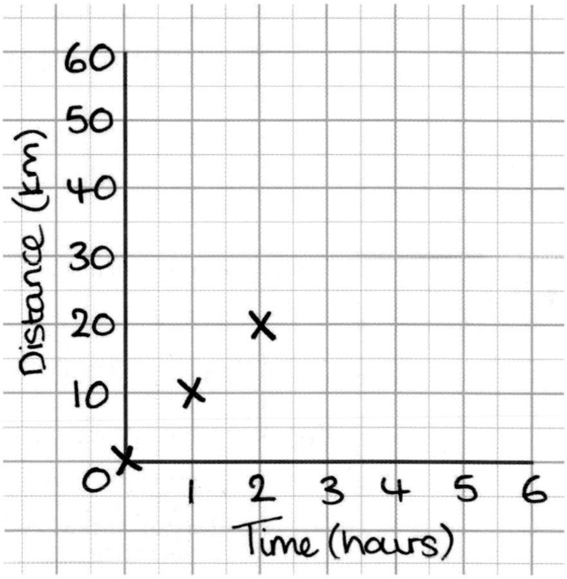

Task

1. Copy and complete Lucy's table.
2. Copy and complete Lucy's graph.
3. How far does Lucy run in $1\frac{1}{2}$ hours?
4. How long does it take Lucy to run 35 km?

Pete runs at 12 kilometres per hour.

5. Copy and complete this formula for Pete.

   Distance = ☐ × time

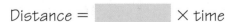

6. Make a table for this formula.
7. Draw a graph of Pete's distance against time.

How far does Pete run in $1\frac{1}{2}$ hours?
How long does it take Pete to run 36 km?

Exercise

SU

1 Look at this sign.

PICK YOUR OWN STRAWBERRIES

JUST

£2 per kilogram

(a) Copy and complete this formula. *w* stands for the weight of the strawberries in kilograms.

Cost (£) = ▨ × *w*

(b) Copy this table. Use the formula to complete it.

Weight (kg)	0	1	2	3	4	5	6
Weight ×2	0				8		
Cost (£)	0				8		

(c) Copy the graph. Use your table to complete it.

(d) Join your points with a straight line.

(e) How much does it cost for 3.5 kg of strawberries?

(f) John spends £9 on strawberries. How many kilograms does he buy?

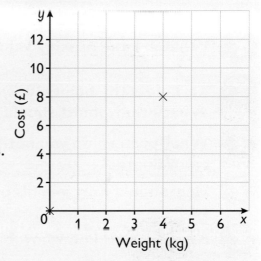

SU

2 The formula for the perimeter of this rectangle is:

Perimeter (m) = 2 × Length + 10

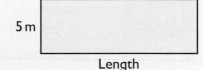

5 m

Length

(a) Copy this table. Use the formula to complete it.

Length (m)	0	1	2	3	4	5	6
Length ×2	0			6			12
+10	+10	+10	+10	+10	+10	+10	+10
Perimeter (m)	10			16			22

(b) Draw a graph of perimeter against length.

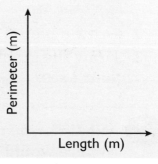

Tables of values

Complete this table of values for the graph of y = x + 2.

Mr Smith

How do I do that?

Karl

Here is the table.

x	0	1	2	3	4
+2	+2	+2		+2	
$y = x + 2$	2			5	

? What are the missing values?

? Karl plots the points (0, 2) and (3, 5). What other points should Karl plot?

? What pattern do you notice in the co-ordinates?

? How should Karl join his points?

? How did Karl know how big to make his axes?

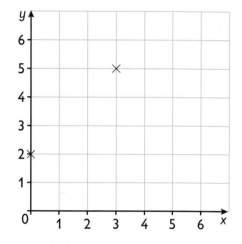

Task

I Copy and complete these tables.

x	0	1	2	3	4
+1	+1	+1	+1	+1	+1
$y = x + 1$	1		3		

x	0	1	2	3	4
+3	+3			+3	
$y = x + 3$	3			6	

x	0	1	2	3	4
+4	+4		+4		
$y = x + 4$			6		

x	0	1	2	3	4
+5	+5				+5
$y = x + 5$					9

2 Draw a pair of axes. Take x from 0 to 4 and y from 0 to 9.

3 Draw the graphs of $y = x + 1$, $y = x + 3$, $y = x + 4$ and $y = x + 5$ on your axes.

? What do you notice about your graphs?
Where would the lines $y = x + 2$ and $y = x + 6$ go?

Exercise

1 For each part of this question
   (i) copy and complete the table
   (ii) write down the largest and smallest x and y co-ordinates
   (iii) draw the graph.

(a)

x	0	1	2	3	4
$+7$	$+7$	$+7$	$+7$	$+7$	$+7$
$y = x + 7$	7				

(b)

x	1	2	3	4	5
-1	-1	-1	-1	-1	-1
$y = x - 1$	0			3	

2 Michelle wants to draw the graph of $y = 2x$.

Each y co-ordinate will be double the x co-ordinate.

Michelle

(a) Copy and complete Michelle's table.

x	0	1	2	3	4
$\times 2$	$\times 2$	$\times 2$	$\times 2$	$\times 2$	$\times 2$
$y = 2x$	0			6	

(b) Draw the graph of $y = 2x$.

3 **(a)** Make a table like the one in question 2 for the graph of $y = 4x$.
   (b) Draw the graph of $y = 4x$.

4 Draw the graph of $y = x$.

$y = x$ means the y co-ordinates are the same as the x co-ordinates.

Finishing off

Now that you have finished this chapter you should be able to:

- spot patterns in the co-ordinates of a straight line
- use a formula to draw a graph
- make a table of values to draw a graph.

Review exercise

1 (a) Write down the co-ordinates of the points marked on each of these lines.

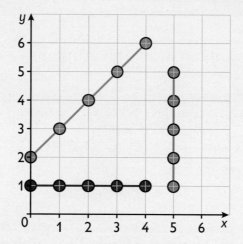

(b) What pattern do you notice for each line?

(c) Match each line to its equation.

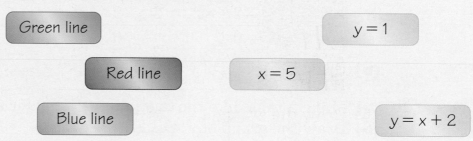

Green line		$y = 1$
Red line	$x = 5$	
Blue line		$y = x + 2$

2 (a) Draw a pair of axes from 0 to 6.

(b) Plot the points $(0, 0)$, $(1, 1)$, $(2, 2)$, $(3, 3)$ and $(6, 6)$.

(c) Join the points with a straight line.

(d) Write down the co-ordinates of another point on your line.

(e) What pattern do you notice?

3 Look at this sign.

(a) Copy and complete this formula.
w stands for the weight of the apples in kilograms.

Cost (pence) = ⬜⬜⬜ × w

Apples only **16p** per kilogram

(b) Copy this table.
Use the formula to complete it.

Weight (kg)	0	1	2	3	4	5
Cost = Weight ×16 (p)	0		32		64	

(c) Follow these steps to draw a graph of cost against weight.

(i) Copy and complete this list of co-ordinates.

$(0, 0)$, $(1,$ ⬜ $)$, $(2, 32)$, $(3,$ ⬜ $)$,

$(4, 64)$, $(5,$ ⬜ $)$

(ii) Plot your points on a pair of axes.

(iii) Join the points with a straight line.

(d) How much does it cost for 2.5 kg of apples?

(e) Tim spends 72p on apples.
How many kilograms does he buy?

4 Megan wants to draw the graph of $y = 2x + 1$.

(a) Copy and complete Megan's table.

x	0	1	2	3	4
$2x$	0			+6	
+1	+1	+1	+1	+1	+1
$y = 2x + 1$	1			7	

(b) Draw the graph of $y = 2x + 1$.

5 (a) Make a table like the one in question 4 for the graph of $y = 2x + 2$.

(b) Draw the graph of $y = 2x + 2$.

Answers

Here are the answers to the 'Finishing off' Review exercises to help you check your progress. All other answers are in the Teacher's Resource that goes with this book.

1 Co-ordinates (page 8)

1 3rd quadrant, 4th quadrant, 2nd quadrant, 1st quadrant
2 A(1, 3), B(−1, 1), C(−5, −3), D(3, 0), E(0, 6), F(0, −4), G(2, −3), H(5, −2), J(−3, −4), K(−6, 5)
3 **(a)**, **(b)** and **(c)**

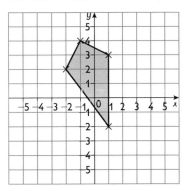

(d) A kite

2 Numbers (pages 18–19)

1 **(i)** **(a)** 4200   four thousand two hundred
    (b) 420   four hundred and twenty
    (c) 42   forty two
  (ii) The digits move one place to the left OR the numbers have been divided by 10 each time.
  (iii) **(a)** 4280   four thousand two hundred and eighty
    (b) 500   five hundred
    (c) 122   one hundred and twenty two
2 **(a)** 97 653
  (b) 0.35679
  (c) Any numbers, including decimals, between the lowest (60 357 and 60 357.9) and the highest (69 753).
  (d) Any two numbers using the given digits, e.g. 67.5 and 6.75.

3

×1000	23 000	3 000 000	4 610 000	2 750 000	4 200 000
×100	2300	300 000	46 100	275 000	420 000
×10	230	30 000	4 610	27 500	42 000
Number	23	3 000	461	2 750	4 200
÷10	2.3	300	46.1	275	420
÷100	0.23	30	4.61	27.5	42
÷1000	0.023	3	0.461	2.75	4.2

4 **(a)** 72 000   **(b)** 73 000
  (c) 76 000   **(d)** 77 000
  (e) 79 000

5

Number	Nearest 10	Nearest 100	Nearest 1000
2 587	2 590	2 600	3 000
9 449	9 450	9 400	9 000
16 508	16 510	16 500	17 000
12 473	12 470	12 500	12 000
47 900	47 900	47 900	48 000

6 Accept answers ±2 °C
  (a) 145 °C
  (b) **(i)** 175 °C   **(ii)** 108 °C
  (c) **(i)** 68 °C–74 °C   **(ii)** 84 °C–91 °C

3 Angles (pages 28–29)

1 **(b)**, **(c)** A 60°, acute
        B 33°, acute
        C 130°, obtuse
        D 207°, reflex
2 Ask your teacher to check your angles.
3 A = 80°   B = 95°   C = 50°
4 X = 138°   Y = 48°   Z = 35°
5 **(a)** Castleton
  (b) Bradwell
  (c) Peak Forest
  (d) Bradwell, Eyam and Stoney Middleton

4 Displaying data (pages 38–39)

1 **(a)**

Magazine	Tally
Pop star	ⵏⵏⵏ ⵏ
Mizzi	ⵏⵏⵏ
Teen idol	ⵏⵏⵏ
Chat	ⵏⵏⵏ

  (b) Ask your teacher to check your bar chart.
2 **(a)** **(i)** With Grow-well 5.7, without Grow-well 4.9 (4.857 14 rounded up)
    (ii) With Grow-well 5, without Grow-well 5
  (b) Yes
  (c) The mean
3

4 **(a)** **(i)** 3   **(ii)** not a mistake   **(iii)** 7
  (b) **(i)** 10 g   **(ii)** a mistake   **(iii)** 4 g
  (c) **(i)** 166   **(ii)** a mistake   **(iii)** 5
5 **(a)** **(i)** 26.1 °C   **(ii)** 11 °C

5 Decimals (pages 48–49)

1 **(a)** **(i)** 4.3   **(ii)** 0.7   **(iii)** 10.8
  (b) **(i)** 0.06   **(ii)** 0.37   **(iii)** 1.21
  (c) **(i)** 0.37   **(ii)** 7.46
2 **(a)** **(i)** 52   **(ii)** 71   **(iii)** 135
  (b) **(i)** 99   **(ii)** 101   **(iii)** 110
3 **(a)** 6.11   **(b)** 0.41   **(c)** 0.18   **(d)** 1.01
4 **(a)** 26.08 kg, 26.23 kg, 26.61 kg, 27.1 kg, 27.44 kg
  (b) 13.02 m, 13.2 m, 13.28 m, 13.3 m, 13.34 m
5 **(a)** £40.94   **(b)** 47.07 m   **(c)** 53.3
  (d) £7.25   **(e)** 7.53 m   **(f)** 6.26
6 **(a)** 3.9   **(b)** 5.2   **(c)** 2.7
  (d) 4.1   **(e)** 1.3
7 Numbers which round to 6 are 6.1 to 6.4.
  Numbers which round to 7 are 6.5 to 6.9 and 7.1 to 7.4.

8

Price	Nearest 10p	Nearest £1	Nearest £10
£26.72	£26.70	£27.00	£30
£83.44	£83.40	£83.00	£80
£15.45	£15.50	£15.00	£20
£15.55	£15.60	£16.00	£20

9 **(a)** £2.50 **(b)** £25 **(c)** £12.50 **(d)** £250
10 **(a)** £28.90 **(b)** £34.68 **(c)** £40.46
11 **(a)** £2.37 **(b)** £2.38 **(c)** £3.62

6 Formulae (pages 60–61)
1 **(a)** Cost (£) = $4 + 5 \times$ number of hours
   (b) **(i)** £9 **(ii)** £14 **(iii)** £19
2 **(a)** 1 **(b)** 8 **(c)** 0 **(d)** 5
3 **(a)** a stands for the number of adults,
   c stands for the number of children.
   (b) £22
4 **(a)** **(i)** 7 **(ii)** 7
   (b) Yes
5 **(a)** 6 **(b)** 9 **(c)** $3 \times n$
6 **(a)** **(i)** Cost (pence) = $15 \times 5 + 50 \times 4 = 275\text{p} = £2.75$
   (ii) Cost (pence) = $15 \times 3 + 50 \times 7 = 395\text{p} = £3.95$
   (b) Cost (pence) = $15c + 50d$
   (c) $210\text{p} = £2.10$
7 **(a)** Cost = $15s$
   (b) Tim bought 6 snakes, Meena bought 4 snakes,
   Mark bought 8 snakes.

7 Construction (pages 70–71)
1 **(i)** Ask your teacher to check your constructions.
   (ii) **(a)** 55°, 7.5 cm and 9.5 cm
      (b) 85°, 35° and 6 cm
      (c) 31°, 20° and 129°
2 **(a)** Ask your teacher to check your scale drawing.
   (b) 10 km
3 Ask your teacher to check your construction.
   4.2 cm, 4.2 cm and 90°

8 Real-life graphs (pages 78–79)
1 **(a)** Ask your teacher to check your graph.
   (b) End of March
   (c) End of August
   (d) August. This is holiday time.
   (e) February, March, May, July, September, October, November
   (f) June **(g)** £33 **(h)** £9
2 **(a)** Ask your teacher to check your graph.
   (b) €2.10 **(c)** £3.33
   (d) €0.90 **(e)** Harry
3 **(a)** 720 m **(b)** 270 m **(c)** 2 minutes
   (d) 450 m **(e)** After 7 minutes **(f)** 4 minutes
   (g) Alan's
   (h) After 8 minutes. When she gets faster, the line gets steeper.

9 Working with directed numbers (pages 86–87)
1 **(a)** +2 minutes **(b)** −1 minutes **(c)** −3 minutes
   (d) +5 minutes **(e)** +15 minutes **(f)** −30 minutes
2 **(a)** Fast: 2 minutes.
   (b) Slow: 1 minute.
   (c) Slow: 4 minutes.
3 Wednesday
4 **(a)** −1 **(b)** −3 **(c)** +1 **(d)** −5
   (e) −3 **(f)** −8 **(g)** −7 **(h)** −2
   (i) −11 **(j)** +1

5 **(a)** +5 **(b)** −18 **(c)** −12 **(d)** −11
   (e) +3 **(f)** +2 **(g)** −11 **(h)** −19
   (i) −6 **(j)** −8
6 **(a)** −2 **(b)** 2 **(c)** −3
   (d) −1 **(e)** 5 **(f)** −4
   (g) −14 **(h)** −3 **(i)** −1
7 **(a)** −3 **(b)** −3 **(c)** −8
   (d) −7 **(e)** −5 **(f)** −13
   (g) +9 **(h)** +7 **(i)** −6
8 **(a)** −15.3 **(b)** −19.2 **(c)** 468 **(d)** −100
   (e) 65.7 **(f)** 29.6 **(g)** 12.6 **(h)** −68.7
9 **(a)** $0 + 3 = +3$
   (b) $3 - 2 = +1$
   (c) $+1 + 1 = +2$ $+2 - 4 = -2$
      $-2 + 3 = +1$ $+1 - 4 = -3$
      $-3 + 2 = -1$ $-1 - 3 = -4$
      $-4 + 5 = +1$ $+1 - 4 = -3$
      $-3 + 1 = -2$ $-2 - 4 = -6$
      $-6 + 6 = 0$
   (d) Mark wins. The last move is unnecessary, the game is over.

10 Fractions (pages 96–97)
1 **(a)** $\frac{1}{2} = \frac{5}{10}$ **(b)** $\frac{2}{3} = \frac{6}{9}$ **(c)** $\frac{1}{3} = \frac{5}{15}$ **(d)** $\frac{3}{5} = \frac{6}{10}$
2 **(a)** $\frac{1}{8} + \frac{3}{8} = \frac{4}{8} = \frac{1}{2}$
   (b) $\frac{5}{12} + \frac{1}{12} = \frac{6}{12} = \frac{1}{2}$
   (c) $\frac{1}{8} + \frac{5}{8} = \frac{6}{8} = \frac{3}{4}$
   (d) $\frac{7}{12} + \frac{1}{12} = \frac{8}{12} = \frac{2}{3}$
   (e) $\frac{5}{9} + \frac{2}{9} = \frac{7}{9}$
3 **(a)** **(i)** $20\% \times 15 = £3$ **(ii)** $£15 - £3 = £12$
   (b) **(i)** $20\% \times £35 = £7$ **(ii)** $£35 - £7 = £28$
   (c) **(i)** $20\% \times £40 = £8$ **(ii)** $£40 - £8 = £32$
4

Fraction	Decimal	Percentage
$\frac{13}{100}$	0.13	13%
$\frac{57}{100}$	0.57	57%
$\frac{33}{100}$	0.33	33%

5 **(a)**

$\frac{3}{8} = \frac{1}{2}$	$\frac{1}{2} \times 50 = 25$	$\frac{1}{2} = 0.2$	$\frac{6}{12} = \frac{1}{2}$
$\frac{3}{4} = 75\%$	$\frac{1}{5} + \frac{2}{5} = \frac{3}{10}$	$\frac{2}{3} \times 15 = 10$	$\frac{1}{12} + \frac{2}{12} = \frac{3}{12} = \frac{1}{3}$
$\frac{2}{5} \times 10 = 2$	$\frac{6}{8} = \frac{3}{4}$	$\frac{6}{9} = \frac{1}{3}$	$\frac{1}{4} = 0.25$
$\frac{2}{11} + \frac{5}{11} = \frac{7}{11}$	$\frac{1}{10} = 1\%$	$\frac{3}{10} + \frac{1}{10} = \frac{4}{10} = \frac{2}{5}$	$\frac{3}{4} \times 12 = 8$

   (b) $\frac{1}{2}$

11 Units (pages 104–105)
1

		Metric	Imperial
Length		millimetres	inches
		centimetres	feet
		metres	yards
		kilometres	miles
Weight (mass)		grams	ounces
		kilograms	pounds
			stones
Capacity (volume)		millilitres	pints
		litres	

2 **(a)** **(i)** 16   **(ii)** 14
    (b) $1\frac{1}{2}$ stones, 1 stone 4 lb, 12 lb, 180 oz, 176 oz, 10 lb 13 oz
3 **(a)** Meena weighs 6 stone 6 lb,
       Mr Hill weighs 14 stone 4 lb.
    (b) Meena is 5 feet 2 inches tall,
       Mr Hill is 6 feet 3 inches.
4 **(a)** 10 miles   **(b)** 20 miles   **(c)** 25 miles   **(d)** 35 miles
5 **(a)** 24 kilometres   **(b)** 48 kilometres
    (c) 160 kilometres   **(d)** 320 kilometres
6 **(a)** flour 1 kg   **(b)** baby 6 kg   **(c)** dog 25 kg
    (d) girl 50 kg   **(e)** apple 100 g   **(f)** book 450 g

12 Flat shapes (pages 112–113)

1

Shape	How many in pattern?
Right-angled triangle	8
Other isosceles triangle	4
Square	1
Other parallelogram	2
Other trapezium	1
Kite	2

2 Ask your teacher to check your drawing.
3 **(a)** Ask your teacher to check your drawing.
      Parallelogram
    (b) Ask your teacher to check your drawing.
      Trapezium
4 Ask your teacher to check your tessellations.
5

	Name of shape	How many lines of symmetry?
	Rectangle	2
	Square	4
	Parallelogram	0
	Rhombus	2
	Trapezium	0
	Kite	1
	Arrowhead	1

13 Special numbers (pages 122–123)

1 **(a)** Any 5 multiples of 6: for example 6, 12, 18, 24, 30.
    (b) Any 5 out of: 1, 2, 4, 5, 10, 20, 25, 50 and 100.
    (c) Any 5 square numbers, for example 1, 4, 9, 16, 25.
    (d) Any 5 cube numbers, for example 1, 8, 27, 64, 125.
    (e) Any 5 powers of 2, for example 2, 4, 8, 16, 32.

2 It is a multiple of 4.
   One of its factors is 8.
   It is a square number.
   It is a power of 2.

3 **(a)**

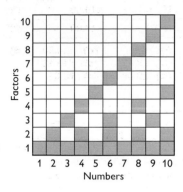

    (b) Diagonal line bottom left to top right shaded, and
      bottom row all shaded. Every other shaded on second
      row.

4 **(a)**

Number	Number of factors
1	1
2	2
3	2
4	3
5	2
6	4
7	2
8	4
9	3
10	4

    (b) 2, 3, 5 and 7
    (c) Prime numbers (can you explain why this is?)
    (d) 1, 4, 9
    (e) Square numbers (can you explain why this is?)
5 **(a)** False (2 is the only even prime number).
    (b) False
    (c) False
    (d) True
    (e) False
    (f) True

14 Doing a survey (pages 130–131)
Ask your teacher to check your work.

15 Ratio and proportion (pages 138–139)

1 **(a)**

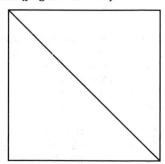

(b)

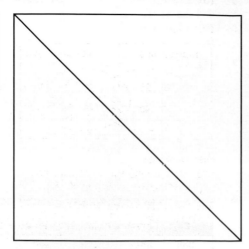

(c)

2 8 egg yolks
600 ml milk
600 ml double cream
260 g chocolate

3 **(a)** £4 **(b)** £10 **(c)** £7

4 **(a)** 10, 20 **(b)** 6, 24 **(c)** 20, 10 **(d)** 12, 18

5 **(a)** 1 : 2 **(b)** 2 : 1 **(c)** 1 : 3
2 : 4 8 : 4 5 : 15
6 : 12 18 : 9 4 : 12
8 : 16 10 : 5 2 : 6
9 : 27

6 **(a)** 5 miles **(b)** 10 miles
(c) 50 miles **(d)** 25 miles
(e) 15 miles **(f)** 30 miles

16 Equations (pages 146–147)

1 **(a)** **(i)** ☐ ← -7 ← 12

(ii) ☐ ← $+4$ ← 1

(iii) ☐ ← -8 ← 16

(iv) ☐ ← $+3$ ← 3

(b) **(i)** 5 **(ii)** 5 **(iii)** 8 **(iv)** 6

2 **(a)** **(i)** ☐ ← $\div 2$ ← 20

(ii) ☐ ← $\times 2$ ← 2

(iii) ☐ ← $\div 4$ ← 4

(iv) ☐ ← $\times 7$ ← 3

(b) **(i)** 10 **(ii)** 4 **(iii)** 1 **(iv)** 21

3 **(a)** $a = 3$ **(b)** $b = 2$ **(c)** $c = 7$
(d) $d = 6$ **(e)** $e = 7$ **(f)** $f = 6$

4 **(a)** $a = 6$ **(b)** $b = 4$ **(c)** $c = 3$
(d) $d = 16$ **(e)** $e = 45$ **(f)** $f = 3$

5 **(a)** $n = 1$ **(b)** $n = 5$ **(c)** $n = 11$
(d) $n = 24$ **(e)** $n = 12$ **(f)** $n = 4$
(g) $n = 14$ **(h)** $n = 1$ **(i)** $n = 4$

6 **(a)** $4n = 28$ **(b)** $n = 7$
(c) $n - 3 = 1$ **(d)** $n = 4$

7 **(a)** 5 kg **(b)** 4 kg
(c) 2 kg **(d)** 3 kg

17 Measuring (pages 154–155)

1 **(a)** $27\,\text{cm}^3$ **(b)** $9\,\text{cm}^2$ **(c)** 6 **(d)** $54\,\text{cm}^2$

2 **(a)** 60 m **(b)** 29 fence panels

3 Floor area = $15.5\,\text{m}^2$
She needs to buy 16 square metres of carpet.

4 **(a)** 10 cm **(b)** $100\,\text{cm}^2$

5 **(a)** $3\,\text{m}^2$ **(b)** 300 cm by 100 cm
(c) $30\,000\,\text{cm}^2$ **(d)** 10 000

18 Percentages (pages 162–163)

1 **(a)** **(i)** $\frac{1}{4}$ **(ii)** 25%

(b) **(i)** $\frac{3}{5}$ **(ii)** 60%

(c) **(i)** $\frac{3}{10}$ **(ii)** 30%

(d) **(i)** $\frac{4}{5}$ **(ii)** 80%

2 **(a)** 10% **(b)** 25% **(c)** 50%
(d) 75% **(e)** 30% **(f)** 90%
(g) 20% **(h)** 80% **(i)** 45%
(j) 44% **(k)** 68% **(l)** 46%

3 **(a)** $\frac{1}{2}$ **(b)** $\frac{1}{4}$ **(c)** $\frac{3}{4}$ **(d)** $\frac{1}{10}$
(e) $\frac{23}{50}$ **(f)** $\frac{19}{25}$ **(g)** $\frac{1}{25}$ **(h)** $\frac{1}{20}$
(i) $\frac{9}{10}$ **(j)** $\frac{9}{20}$ **(k)** $\frac{17}{20}$ **(l)** $\frac{11}{50}$

4 Spark's Electrics is better (= 25% off).

5 **(a)** 630 **(b)** 500 **(c)** 530
     -210 -125 -100
     £420 £375 £430

so **(b)** is cheapest.

6 History 60% Science 56% Maths 70%
English 80% French 65% DT 90%
Tim has done best in DT.

7 Make changes and move
(a) **(i)** Reduction £9
(ii) Reduction £45
(iii) Reduction £105

(b) **(i)** Sale price £21
(ii) Sale price £105
(iii) Sale price £245

19 Symmetry (page 168)

1 **(a)** **(iii)**

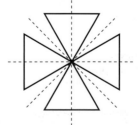

(iv)

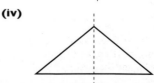

(v)

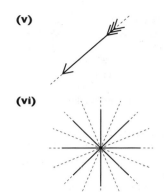

(vi)

(b) (i) Order 2   **(ii)** Order 2
     (iii) Order 4   **(vi)** Order 8
(c) (iii) and **(vi)**

20 Probability (pages 176–177)

1 (a) Evens   **(b)** Certain   **(c)** Unlikely
   (d) Likely   **(e)** Impossible
2 (a) Yes   **(b)** 36   **(c)** 9   **(d)** $\frac{9}{36} = \frac{1}{4}$
   (e) (i) $\frac{3}{36} = \frac{1}{12}$ **(ii)** $\frac{3}{36} = \frac{1}{12}$ **(iii)** $\frac{2}{36} = \frac{1}{18}$ **(iv)** $\frac{1}{36}$
3 (a) No   **(b)** $\frac{5}{100} = 0.05$ **(c)** $\frac{25}{100} = 0.25$
4 (a) 8   **(b)** $\frac{1}{8}$ **(c)** $\frac{5}{8}$ **(d)** $\frac{3}{8}$
5 (a) $\frac{3}{20} = 0.15$
   (b) $\frac{17}{20} = 0.85$
   (c) 6. Any explanation that recognises that the number 3 has to be doubled, as 40 is twice 20.

21 Number patterns (pages 184–185)

1 Possible sequences are:

1	2	3	4	5
1	5	6	10	15
2	4	8	16	32
5	10	15	20	25
1	4	9	16	25
3	6	9	12	15
4	8	12	16	20
2	4	6	8	10

and the same backwards.
2 (a) $t = p \times 3$ **(b)** $t = p + 3$
   (c) $t = p + 5$ **(d)** $t = 5 \times p$
3 Sequence **(a)**
4 (a) Correct   **(b)** Incorrect
   (c) Incorrect   **(d)** Correct
5 (a) D   E (alphabet)
   (b) F   S (days of week)
   (c) J   J (months)
   (d) pentagon   hexagon
   (e) S   SW (compass points)
   (f) 100 thousand   1 million

22 Using numbers (pages 196–197)

1 (a) (i) and **(ii)** 20
   (b) (i) and **(ii)** 16
   (d) (i) and **(ii)** 40
2 (a) $4 \times (5 + 3)$ is bigger than $(4 \times 5) + 3$.
   (b) $6 + (7 \times 3)$ is bigger than $6 + (7 + 3)$.
   (c) $(20 \div 4) + 1$ is bigger than $20 \div (4 + 1)$.
   (d) Both are the same.

3 (a) £32.50   **(b)** £35.00
4 6 packs
5 (a) (b)

Multiples of 5		Multiples of 3
20 25 35 40	15 30 45	12 18 21 24 27 33 36 39 42 48

(c) 15, 30, 45
(d) They are multiples of both 3 and 5 OR they are multiples of 15.

6

	Divisible by				
2	**3**	**5**	**10**	**Other**	
236	2811	140	140	19	
140	723	3000	3000	91	
3000	333	3245	2000	463	
2000	3000	105		173	
844	105	2000			

7 (a) (i) 11   **(ii)** 11 r1
      (iii) 12   **(iv)** 12 r4
   (b) (i) 6   **(ii)** 6 r2
      (iii) 60   **(iv)** 60 r5
   (c) (i) £7.00   **(ii)** £7.09
      (iii) £7.09 r4   **(iv)** £7.08 r5

23 Transformations (pages 202–203)

1 (a)

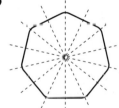

(b) Order 7
(c) 5 lines of symmetry and rotation symmetry of order 5.
2 (a) C: 4 right and 1 up.
   (b) B: clockwise 90° about (3, 1).
   (c) D

3

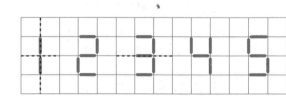

reflection: 2 lines   1 line
rotation: order 2   order 2   order 2

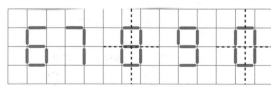

reflection: 2 lines   2 lines
rotation: order 2   order 2

4 1 hexagon
2 order
3 shape
4 reflection
5 translation
6 angles
7 rotation
8 construct
The green squares give the word **heptagon**.

24 Solid shapes (pages 210–211)
I **(a)** **(i)** Stuart   **(ii)** plan
    (b) **(i)** Mary   **(ii)** elevation
    (c) Taj Mahal   **(d)** India
2 **(a)** Two of:

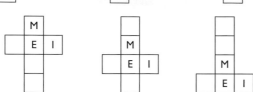

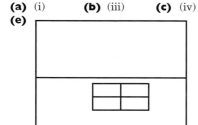

    (d) 3
3 **(a)** (i)   **(b)** (iii)   **(c)** (iv)   **(d)** (ii)
    (e)

25 Drawing graphs (pages 218–219)
I **(a)** Red line: $(0, 1), (1, 1), (2, 1), (3, 1), (4, 1)$
        Blue line: $(5, 1), (5, 2), (5, 3), (5, 4), (5, 5)$
        Green line: $(0, 2), (1, 3), (2, 4), (3, 5), (4, 6)$
   (b) Red line: the y co-ordinate is always 1.
        Blue line: the x co-ordinate is always 5.
        Green line: the y co-ordinate is always 2 more than
        the x co-ordinate.
   (c) Red line: $y = 1$
        Blue line: $x = 5$
        Green line: $y = x + 2$

2 **(a)**, **(b)**, **(c)**, **(d)** Ask your teacher to check your graph
and answers.
   (e) The x co-ordinate is the same as the y co-ordinate.

3 **(a)** Cost (pence) $= 16 \times w$
   (b)

Weight (kg)	0	1	2	3	4	5
Weight ×16	0	16	32	48	64	80
Cost (pence)	0	16	32	48	64	80

   (c) **(i)** $(0, 0), (1, 16), (2, 32), (3, 48), (4, 64), (5, 80)$
        (ii), **(iii)** Ask your teacher to check your graph.
   (d) 40p
   (e) 4.5 kg

4 **(a)**

x	0	1	2	3	4
$2x$	0	2	4	6	8
$+1$	$+1$	$+1$	$+1$	$+1$	$+1$
$y = 2x + 1$	1	3	5	7	9

   (b) Ask your teacher to check your graph.

5 **(a)**

x	0	1	2	3	4
$2x$	0	2	4	6	8
$+2$	$+2$	$+2$	$+2$	$+2$	$+2$
$y = 2x + 2$	2	4	6	8	10

   (b) Ask your teacher to check your graph.